STUDY GUIDE to accompany

Spencer

CONTEMPORARY MACROECONOMICS

Third Edition

Muriel W. Converse
University of Michigan

Worth Publishers, Inc.

Study Guide

to accompany

Spencer: Contemporary Macroeconomics, Third Edition

Copyright © 1975, 1977 by Worth Publishers, Inc.

All rights reserved. No part of this publication may be

reproduced, stored in a retrieval system, or transmitted

in any form or by any means, electronic, mechanical,

photocopying, recording, or otherwise, without the prior

written permission of the publisher

ISBN: 0-87901-076-2

Printed in the United States of America

Third Printing August, 1978

Worth Publishers, Inc.

444 Park Avenue South

New York, New York 10016

To the Student

The purpose of this Study Guide is to help you understand and learn the subject matter in Spencer's *Contemporary Macroeconomics*, 3rd edition; to sharpen your critical faculties; and to provide a convenient guide for review. The chapters in the book correspond to those in the text. In this book you will find:

1. Chapter orientations to convey the major ideas of each chapter and to aid in organizing your thoughts.
2. Fill-in questions (with answers) to help you recall important definitions and concepts.
3. Problems (with answers) to help you develop an understanding of the theoretical material.
4. True–false and multiple-choice questions (with answers) to enable you to test your mastery of each chapter.
5. Learning objectives, which outline what you should be able to do after studying the specific chapter.
6. Discussion questions to stimulate your thinking and make you apply the basic principles of the text.

Before you start, one comment about true–false questions should be made. A statement is said to be *true* only if it is true without exception. If the statement is true under certain (unspecified) assumptions and false under others, that statement is said to be *false*.

In general, this book is designed to help you. You can gain maximum advantage in its use by following three basic procedures:

First, study each chapter assignment in the text until you feel that you have a good overall comprehension of it.

Second, work your way through the corresponding chapter in this book. If there is a section in which you find you are weak, go back to the text and study that section again.

Third, use this book to review and study for examinations. Although this manual is not a substitute for the text, it can be a valuable supplement and complement to it.

ACKNOWLEDGMENTS

It is a pleasure to acknowledge the assistance and cooperation I have received from the many reviewers of this and previous editions. Special thanks go to Professor Allen Early, West Texas State University, for his careful suggestions and attention to detail. Thanks also to George Wright, University of Michigan; Professor Howard Bloch, Thomas S. Karwaki, and Randy S. Numbers, George Mason University; and Professor Donald J. Yankovic and Professor Mike Magura, The University of Texas. Their comments and suggestions have been extraordinarily helpful, but they are in no way responsible for any remaining shortcomings of the book.

Finally, I would like to thank my children, Aaron and Erica, for their careful, if sporadic, help with proofreading.

Muriel W. Converse
Ann Arbor, Michigan
November, 1976

Contents

PART 1

The Problem and Its Setting

Introduction

ORIENTATION

This introduction develops and explains the following concepts:

The definition of economics as a social science, and the distinction between microeconomics and macroeconomics.

Some common types of logical errors or fallacies.

FILL-IN QUESTIONS

Complete the following sentences. (Answers are given at the end of the Introduction.)

1. Economics is a social science concerned chiefly with the way society chooses to employ its _____ _____, which have alternative uses, to produce _____ and _____ for present and future consumption.

2. The branch of economics concerned with the behavior of the specific economic units or parts that make up an economic system is called _____ _____.

   The branch which deals with the economy as a whole or with large segments of it is called _____ _____.

3. A _____ is a representation of the essential features of a theory or of a real-world situation.

PROBLEMS

(Answers are given at the end of the Introduction.)

1. The price of hamburger (*P*) determines the number of pounds of hamburger (*Q*) that people would like to buy during a given period of time. Assume that the relationship is as shown in the table.

P (per pound)	Q (pounds)
$0.30	8
0.40	7
0.50	6
0.60	5
0.70	4

(a) Graph the relationship, putting price on the *Y* (vertical) axis and quantity on the *X* (horizontal) axis.

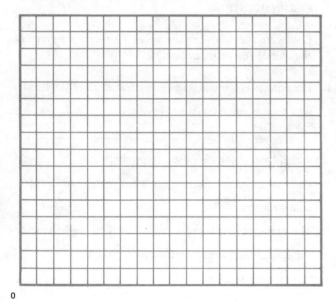

0

(b) The relationship between *P* and *Q* is (direct/inverse) _____.

(c) The slope of a straight line between two points is measured by the change in vertical distance divided by the change in horizontal distance between these points (the "rise" over the "run"). If the curve slopes downward to the right, its slope is negative. If it slopes upward to the right, its slope is positive.

   The slope of the line in part (a) equals _____.

2. You are given the following relationship between two economic variables, *A* and *B*.

A	B
2	9
3	7
4	6
5	8
6	9

(a) Graph the relationship, putting *A* on the *X* axis and *B* on the *Y* axis.

0

(b) The relationship between *A* and *B* is inverse when *A* is between _____ and _____. The relationship is direct when *A* is between _____ and _____.

(c) The coordinates of the point at which *B* is a minimum are (_____, _____).

SELF-TEST: TRUE–FALSE QUESTIONS

Circle T if the statement is true, F if it is false. (Answers are given at the end of the Introduction.)

T F 1. Economics is concerned with the allocation of scarce resources among alternative uses.

T F 2. Since everybody has the capability of supplying

some form of labor services, labor is *not a* scarce resource.

T F 3. Studying the behavior of the output of the economy as a whole is macroeconomics, but studying the behavior of the output of the steel industry is microeconomics.

T F 4. The statement "If my wage increases I am better off; therefore, if all wages go up, everybody must be better off" is an example of the fallacy of division.

T F 5. The statement "High blood pressure and ulcers increase worker productivity because in highly productive economies people generally suffer these maladies" is an example of the fallacy of false cause.

SELF-TEST: MULTIPLE-CHOICE QUESTIONS

Circle the letter that corresponds to the best answer. (Answers are given at the end of the Introduction.)

1. When we say that a resource is scarce, we mean that:
   (a) There is almost none of it.
   (b) It is hard to find.
   (c) It is useful in the production of goods and services.
   (d) There is not as much of it as society would use if society could satisfy all of its wants.
   (e) It is expensive.

2. The statement "Since inflation is harmful to the economy as a whole, rising prices must be harmful to me also" is an example of the fallacy of:
   (a) False cause.
   (b) Composition.

(c) Bad thinking.
(d) Division.
(e) None of the above.

CHECKPOINT: LEARNING OBJECTIVES

At this point, you should be able to do all of the following:

1. Define all of the technical terms and concepts listed at the end of the Introduction in the text.

2. Distinguish between microeconomics and macroeconomics.

3. Define and illustrate each of the following fallacies:
   (a) False cause.
   (b) Composition.
   (c) Division.

4. Graph the relationship between two variables, given the necessary data.

QUESTIONS TO THINK ABOUT

1. "Theories are built on abstractions from reality. Therefore, although a theory may be useful in the abstract, it cannot be useful in explaining reality." Do you agree?

2. Many subjects in economics have both micro- and macroeconomic aspects. To illustrate this, think about the micro- and macroeconomic aspects of:
   (a) Taxation.
   (b) Production.
   (c) Consumption.
   (d) Prices.

Can you give any other examples?

ANSWERS

Answers to Fill-in Questions

1. limited resources
   goods
   services

2. microeconomics
   macroeconomics

3. model

Answers to Problems

1. (a)

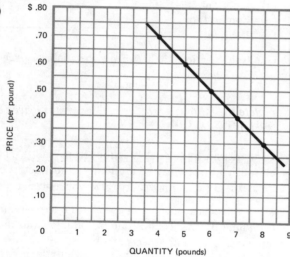

   (b) inverse

   (c) $\dfrac{-0.10}{1} = -0.10$

2. (a)

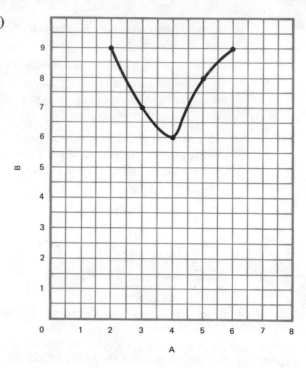

   (b) 2 and 4
   4 and 6

   (c) (4,6)

Answers to True–False Questions

1. T	3. T	5. T
2. F	4. F	

Answers to Multiple-Choice Questions

1. d   2. d

CHAPTER 1

Resources and Goals of Our Economic System

This chapter develops and explains the following concepts:

The different types of resources of an economy.

Four features which facilitate the transformation of a society's resources into output of goods and services.

The goals of our economic system and two reasons why their realization may involve sacrifice.

The law of scarcity and the need to economize.

The three basic economic questions: WHAT, HOW, and FOR WHOM.

The production-possibilities curve, and some of its uses.

FILL-IN QUESTIONS

Complete the following sentences. (Answers are given at the end of the chapter.)

1. The four basic types of resources which a society uses to produce output are called the _____ _____.

2. Remuneration for the use of land is called _____; remuneration for the use of money which business firms borrow to purchase capital goods is called _____; remuneration for the use of labor services is called _____; and remuneration for the services of an entrepreneur is called _____.

3. The division of productive activity among individuals and regions so that no one person or area is self-sufficient is called _____.

4. Specialization by workers is called _____.

5. Anything generally accepted in exchange is called _____.

6. When a production system is fully utilizing its resources in such a manner that no change in the combination of inputs

can be made that will increase the output of one product without decreasing that of another, the production system has attained _____ _____.

7. When an economy is producing the combination of goods that people prefer, given their incomes and the attainment of technical efficiency, that economy is said to have achieved _____ or _____ _____ efficiency.

8. The fact that there are never enough goods and services because economic resources are scarce and can be increased, if at all, only through effort or sacrifice is known as the _____.

9. An economy in which government exercises primary control over decisions concerning what and how much to produce is called a _____ economy; an economy in which the three basic economic questions are answered by the interaction of supply and demand in competitive markets is called a _____ economy; and an economy in which the three basic economic questions are answered partially by free markets and partially by central governmental authority is called a _____ economy.

10. A graph showing the different combinations of two goods that an economy can produce, given fixed amounts of fully and (technically) efficiently utilized resources and a fixed state of technological knowledge, is called a _____ _____.

11. If, in a given state of technology, resources are in fixed supply, fully and efficiently utilized, and can be used in the production of two goods, then, to produce additional units of one good, society must give up increasing amounts of the other good. This is known as the law of _____ _____.

PROBLEMS

(Answers are given at the end of the chapter.)

1. The four assumptions underlying the production-possibilities schedule or curve are:

   (a) _____
   _____
   _____

   (b) _____
   _____
   _____

   (c) _____
   _____
   _____

   (d) _____
   _____
   _____

2. The production-possibilities schedule shows: _____
   _____
   _____
   _____
   _____

3. The law of increasing costs states: _____
   _____
   _____
   _____
   _____

4. Costs in the above sense increase because: _____
   _____
   _____
   _____
   _____
   _____
   _____

5. You are given the following production-possibilities schedule.

Capital goods	Consumer goods	Sacrifice of consumer goods for capital goods	Sacrifice of capital goods for consumer goods
0	18	———	———
1	17	———	———
2	15	———	———
3	11	———	———
4	6	———	
5	0		

(a) Fill in the last two columns of the table.

(b) From this table we see that to obtain additional units of capital goods, we must sacrifice _____ _____ amounts of consumer goods, and to obtain additional units of consumer goods, we must sacrifice _____ _____ amounts of capital goods.

(c) Graph the production-possibilities curve from the data in the table.

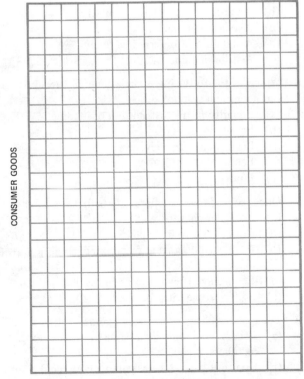

CAPITAL GOODS

CONSUMER GOODS

(d) Show a point, *I*, at which society would be using its resources in a technically inefficient manner.

(e) From point *I* we can see that when society uses its resources more efficiently, it is possible to have more of _____ goods.

(f) On the same graph, put a new production-possibilities curve that reflects economic growth. Does the new curve have to be parallel to the old one? _____

(g) The production-possibilities curve will shift out more over time, the (more/less) _____ society allocates resources to the production of capital goods.

The real cost of growth is thus seen as the _____ _____ of present consumption goods. But growth enables a society to have more of _____ .

SELF-TEST: TRUE–FALSE QUESTIONS

Circle T if the statement is true, F if it is false. (Answers are given at the end of the chapter.)

T F 1. Economic resources consist of property resources and human resources.

T F 2. Capital as a factor of production consists of funds owned or borrowed to buy capital goods.

T F 3. If total wages increase and total profits fall, there has been a change in the functional distribution of income.

T F 4. If capital widening occurs, capital deepening must occur.

T F 5. By "specialization," economists mean not only specialization of skills by people but also specialization in production by regions.

T F 6. There is likely to be less specialization in a barter economy than there is in an economy that uses money as a medium of exchange.

T F 7. If an economy is technically efficient, it must also be allocatively (economically) efficient.

T F 8. If an economy transfers resources from the production of cameras to the production of chairs and gets four additional chairs while giving up only two cameras, that economy could not have been technically efficient before the transfer.

T F 9. An economy can be economically efficient even if it is not fully utilizing available resources.

T F 10. By an equitable distribution of income, we mean that income must be distributed equally among all individuals in society.

T F 11. If the resources of a society were all equally suitable for and efficient in producing all products, the society would not have to give up increasing amounts of one product to get additional units of the other.

T F 12. If the resources of an economy are not fully utilized, the economy will not be at a point on its production-possibilities curve.

T F 13. An economy can reach a point outside its production-possibilities curve if it uses its resources more efficiently.

SELF-TEST: MULTIPLE-CHOICE QUESTIONS

Circle the letter that corresponds to the best answer. (Answers are given at the end of the chapter.)

1. Which of the following is *not* a factor of production?
   (a) Land.
   (b) Money.
   (c) Labor.
   (d) Entrepreneurship.
   (e) They are all factors of production.

2. We say that capital formation occurs in an economy whenever:
   (a) The money supply increases.
   (b) The supply of machinery and equipment increases.
   (c) The amount of money that people want to borrow to buy capital goods increases.
   (d) The state of technology changes.
   (e) Total output changes.

3. Capital widening is defined as:
   (a) Building larger pieces of equipment.
   (b) Increasing the amount of capital of a given kind that each worker has to work with.
   (c) Increasing the capital stock without changing the quantity or quality of capital that each worker has to work with.
   (d) Increasing labor productivity by increasing the amount of all factors of production that labor has to work with.
   (e) Changing the type of capital in use.

4. One shortcoming of specialization is that it may tend to result in:
   (a) Labor alienation.
   (b) Reduced efficiency.
   (c) Reduced productivity.
   (d) Reduced capital formation.
   (e) Reduced output.

5. By "barter" we mean:
   (a) Bargaining between buyers and sellers in the marketplace.
   (b) Competitive bidding on the part of buyers for the same product.
   (c) Competition on the part of the sellers in the marketplace.
   (d) Direct swapping of one type of good for another.
   (e) Trading goods now with payment to be made in the future.

6. Money is:
   (a) Anything generally acceptable in trade.
   (b) Backed by gold and/or silver.
   (c) Made of paper.
   (d) Never useful for anything but exchange.
   (e) Something that never loses value.

7. Which of the following is *not* a function of money?
   (a) A medium of exchange.
   (b) A means for capital accumulation.
   (c) A measure of value.
   (d) A standard of deferred payment.
   (e) A store of value.

8. Which of the following is *not* a generally accepted goal of our economic system?
   (a) Equality in the distribution of income.
   (b) Economic growth.
   (c) Economic efficiency.
   (d) Economic stability.
   (e) Equity.

9. One result of the law of scarcity is that:
   (a) Goods are never free.
   (b) Goods tend to be expensive.
   (c) In determining what to produce, choices must be made.
   (d) Economic efficiency is not possible.
   (e) Some people must be poor.

10. The question "For whom shall goods be produced?":
   (a) Asks how income shall be distributed among members of society.
   (b) Does not have to be asked in a command economy.
   (c) Does not have to be asked in a market economy.

(d) Has to be asked only in poor societies.

(e) Is never asked in rich societies.

11. The question "How shall goods be produced?":
    (a) Does not have to be answered in a very rich economy because people can have so much of everything.
    (b) Is, in fact, rarely considered, much less answered.
    (c) Must be answered every time a production decision is made.
    (d) Really asks the question "How do people decide what to produce?"
    (e) Does not have to be answered in an economy that does not have an advanced technology.

12. Which of the following statements is most correct?
    (a) To produce more of one good, an economy must give up some other goods.
    (b) To produce more of one good, an economy must give up some other goods if resources are fully and efficiently employed.
    (c) To produce more of one good, an economy must give up some other goods if resources are fully and efficiently employed and if technology is fixed.
    (d) To produce more of one good, an economy must give up some other goods, assuming that resources are fully and efficiently employed, that resources can be shifted from the production of one good into the production of another, and that technology is fixed.
    (e) All of the above are equally correct.

CHECKPOINT: LEARNING OBJECTIVES

At this point, you should be able to do all of the following:

1. Describe the four factors of production and state what the remuneration for the use of each is called.

2. Distinguish between the functional distribution of income and the personal distribution of income.

3. Explain how each of the following facilitates the operation of an economic system:
   (a) Technological progress and capital formation.
   (b) Specialization and exchange.
   (c) The availability of a suitable form of money.
   (d) An environment conducive to economic advancement.

4. Describe the four goals of any economic system, and explain why their realization may involve sacrifices.

5. Distinguish between technical and economic efficiency.

6. Explain why scarcity exists in all societies.

7. List and explain the three fundamental questions that all economic systems must answer.

8. List the four assumptions underlying a production-possibilities schedule or curve.

9. Graph a production-possibilities curve, given a production-possibilities schedule, and explain:
   (a) Whether or not the curve indicates the optimum combination of two goods to produce.
   (b) Why increasing amounts of one good must be sacrificed to get additional units of the other.

10. Calculate the amount of one good that must be given up to get additional units of the other, given a production-possibilities schedule or curve.

11. Given a production-possibilities curve, show:
    (a) A point at which society is underutilizing its resources.
    (b) How economic growth affects its position.

12. Using a production-possibilities curve, explain why a society which devotes some of its resources to capital goods can have more of both capital goods and consumer goods in the future.

QUESTIONS TO THINK ABOUT

1. "Although money is not productive per se, it permits an economy to be more productive than it would be if barter prevailed." Why?

2. Does it make sense to say that resources are scarce when labor is frequently unemployed?

3. In what way or ways does technological change permit society's production possibilities to increase?

4. "It makes sense to talk about the *real* cost of producing additional units of a particular product only if resources are fully and efficiently employed." Do you agree?

5. "An economy that devotes a good part of its resources to capital goods must be shortsighted because people cannot eat machines." Is this statement true?

6. Would the concept of a production-possibilities curve be useful in a command economy? Why or why not?

7. Why would a command economy have to be concerned with the same basic economic questions as a market economy? Would providing answers to these questions involve the use of resources in a command economy? In a market economy?

ANSWERS

Answers to Fill-in Questions

1. factors of production

2. rent
   interest
   wages
   profit

3. specialization

4. division of labor

5. money

6. technical efficiency

7. economic
   allocative

8. law of scarcity

9. command
   market
   mixed

10. production-possibilities curve

11. increasing costs

Answers to Problems

1. (a) The economy produces only two types of goods.
   (b) The same resources can be used to produce both types of goods and can be shifted freely between them.
   (c) The supply of resources and the state of technological knowledge are fixed.
   (d) Society's resources are fully employed in the most (technically) efficient way.

2. The production-possibilities schedule shows the different *combinations* of two goods a society can produce under the four assumptions above.

3. The law of increasing costs states that if the above assumptions are made, a society can get more units of one good only by giving up increasing amounts of the other good.

4. Costs in the above sense increase because the economy's factors of production differ in quality and hence are not all equally suitable for producing the two types of goods. As we transfer resources from the production of one good into another, we tend to transfer them from where they are more productive to where they are less productive. Hence, as we try to get more of one type of good, its real (sacrifice) cost increases.

5. (a)

Sacrifice of consumer goods for capital goods	Sacrifice of capital goods for consumer goods
– 1	– 1
– 2	$-\frac{1}{2}$
– 4	$-\frac{1}{4}$
– 5	$-\frac{1}{5}$
– 6	$-\frac{1}{6}$

(*Note*: To arrive at the figures in the second column, we see that if the economy is producing no consumer goods and we transfer resources away from capital goods, when we give up 1 unit of capital goods we get 6 units of consumer goods. Thus, to get 1 unit of consumer goods, we need give up only $\frac{1}{6}$ of a unit of capital goods.)

(b) increasing
    increasing

(c), (d), (f)

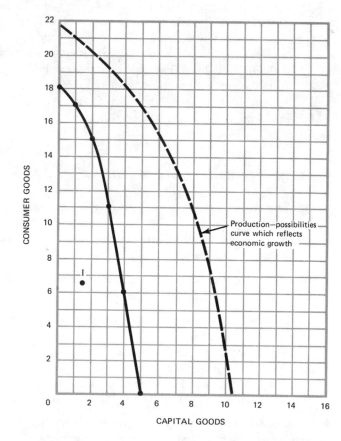

(e) both

(f) no

(g) more
    sacrifice
    both goods

Answers to True–False Questions

1. T	6. T	10. F
2. F	7. F	11. T
3. T	8. F	12. T
4. F	9. F	13. F
5. T		

Answers to Multiple-Choice Questions

1. b	5. d	9. c
2. b	6. a	10. a
3. c	7. b	11. c
4. a	8. a	12. d

CHAPTER 2

Capitalism and Our Mixed Economy

CHAPTER ORIENTATION

This chapter develops and explains the following concepts:

The definition and fundamental institutions of capitalism.

Some criticisms of the capitalist system.

The circular-flow model of economic activity, which represents a broad overview of the operation of a capitalistic economic system.

FILL-IN QUESTIONS

Complete the following sentences. (Answers are given at the end of the chapter.)

1. Capitalism is a system of economic organization characterized by _____ ownership of the means of _____ and _____ _____, and their operation for _____ under predominantly _____ _____ conditions.

2. The right of individuals to transfer assets in a capitalistic economy derives from the institution of _____ _____.

3. The principle of the _____ _____ expresses the idea that if each individual is permitted to pursue his own best interest, he will, in fact, achieve the best good for society.

4. We use the concept of _____ to express the idea that each individual in a capitalistic society is motivated by economic forces and will always act

in such a way as to obtain the greatest amount of satisfaction for the least amount of sacrifice or cost.

5. Rivalry among buyers and sellers of goods and resources is called _____.

6. Competition in a particular market will be greater when there are (many/few) _____ buyers and sellers and when entry into and exit from that market are (least/most) _____ restricted.

7. To express the idea of freedom from government intervention, we use the term _____.

8. In a capitalistic economy, the allocation of goods and services among people and of resources among alternative uses is determined by the _____ system.

9. The American economy is neither a pure market economy nor a pure command economy but is, in fact, a _____ _____ economy.

10. A pure market economy will tend toward equilibrium in the sense that an equivalent combination of monetary and nonmonetary rewards will accrue to any resource in all of its possible uses. This is called the law of _____ _____.

11. The expression _____ _____ refers to the condition which exists when a corporation is not managed by its owners.

12. When there is an efficient distribution of resources between private and public goods, the economy is said to be in _____ balance.

13. An economic system in which the government, through a preconceived plan, plays a primary role in directing the allocation of resources is called a _____ economy.

14. The model that shows the movements of goods, resources, payments, and expenditures between different sectors of the economy is called the _____ _____.

15. Markets in which goods and services are sold are called _____ markets, whereas markets in which the factors of production are bought and sold are called _____ markets.

Circle T if the statement is true, F if it is false. (Answers are given at the end of the chapter.)

T F 1. We are really *not* correct in calling the economic system of the United States capitalistic, because in a capitalist economic system there is no government interference in the economy.

T F 2. A capitalist economy does not require the institution of private property as long as markets are competitive.

T F 3. The principle of the invisible hand introduced by Adam Smith states that because men are basically motivated by benevolence, they will achieve the best good for society.

T F 4. If people decide that they want less of a good than they did previously, the market for that good will adjust so that less of it will be produced.

T F 5. The law of equal advantage states that in equilibrium all occupations pay the same monetary wage.

T F 6. In our economy the law of equal advantage tends not to operate, but resource immobilities often produce a better allocation of resources than would exist if it did operate well.

T F 7. The basic institutions of capitalism tend to cause inequality in the distributions of income and wealth.

T F 8. The separation of ownership and control increases economic efficiency because professional managers usually have a broader perspective than do owner managers and are less likely to abuse their power.

T F 9. Everybody agrees that social imbalance really does exist in the U.S. economy.

T F 10. A planned economy must be a command economy.

T F 11. There are only two sets of markets in the circular-flow model, and this is true whether we include or exclude the government sector.

T F 12. What to produce is decided in the product markets and how to produce is decided in the resource markets.

T F 13. The circular-flow model gives useful insights into the problems of recession and inflation.

SELF-TEST: MULTIPLE-CHOICE QUESTIONS

Circle the letter that corresponds to the best answer. (Answers are given at the end of the chapter.)

1. Pure capitalism is a type of economic system in which:
   (a) The institution of private property exists.
   (b) People are motivated in their economic decisions by self-interest.
   (c) There is economic individualism and a price system.
   (d) There are many buyers and sellers in all markets.
   (e) All of the above are true.

2. Which of the following is *not* a basic institution of capitalism?
   (a) Self-interest.
   (b) Private property.
   (c) Absence of government intervention in all aspects of the economy.
   (d) Free markets.
   (e) All of the above are basic institutions.

3. The "invisible hand" means that:
   (a) The allocation of resources is guided to some extent by the government but in such a way that it is not apparent.
   (b) Men are guided through self-interest to produce the goods and services that society wants.
   (c) Social values push people quietly into suitable professions.
   (d) People will not attempt to be monopolists because they are better off in competitive markets.
   (e) In a competitive system, providence assures a living wage to all.

4. Competition tends to be more intense:
   (a) The greater the number of buyers and sellers in the market and the greater the degree of freedom with which they can enter and leave particular markets.

   (b) The smaller the number of buyers and sellers in the market and the smaller the degree of freedom with which they can enter and leave particular markets.
   (c) The greater the number of buyers and sellers in the market and the smaller the degree of freedom with which they can enter and leave particular markets.
   (d) The smaller the number of buyers and sellers in the market and the greater the degree of freedom with which they can enter and leave particular markets.
   (e) The more patentable is the product produced by industry.

5. The concept "economic man" implies that:
   (a) Man wants to produce the most good for society.
   (b) Man is rational and is motivated by economic forces.
   (c) Man is a product of the economic environment in which he lives.
   (d) Man is economical and tries to save money.
   (e) Man has no concerns except economic ones.

6. If the government followed a policy of complete laissez-faire, this would mean that:
   (a) A judicial system would have to be supplied in the marketplace and would be supplied only if it were profitable.
   (b) People who were unable to afford to buy fire protection from a profit-oriented fire department might have to watch their houses burn down.
   (c) There would be no public education.
   (d) There would be no government projects such as the TVA.
   (e) All of the above are true.

7. If wages are higher in City A than in City B, we can explain this by saying:
   (a) There is disequilibrium in the structure of wages.
   (b) Workers feel that there are nonmonetary advantages to living in City B rather than in City A.
   (c) There are obstacles to movement between Cities A and B.
   (d) Labor is more highly skilled in City A than in City B.
   (e) All of the above are possible explanations.

8. Social imbalance means that:
   (a) Consumers do not know what they want.
   (b) Business firms do not know what consumers want.
   (c) People do not want social goods.
   (d) The distribution of income is very imbalanced—that is, unequal.
   (e) There is a misallocation of resources between the public and private sectors of the economy.

9. In a continuously fully employed economy it is possible to get more social goods only if:

(a) Prices of social goods are increased.

(b) Prices of social goods are reduced.

(c) The degree of competition in the production of social goods is increased.

(d) The production of social goods is subsidized.

(e) The production of private goods is reduced.

10. Which of the following would be a totally unjustified criticism of capitalism?

(a) Even in its purest form it tends to be inefficient.

(b) It tends to result in economic instability.

(c) It may, by concentrating on economic growth, distort society's values.

(d) It tends to produce an unequal distribution of income and wealth.

(e) It tends to produce prolonged periods of unemployment.

11. The model of the circular flow of economic activity presented in the text is:

(a) Applicable to all types of economic systems.

(b) Applicable only to command economies.

(c) Applicable only to market economies.

(d) Not really a model at all.

(e) Microeconomic in nature.

12. If you were a laborer in a factory (as well as a member of a household), then you would be:

(a) A supplier in the product markets and a demander in the resource markets.

(b) A supplier in the product markets and a supplier in the resource markets.

(c) A demander in the product markets and a demander in the resource markets.

(d) A demander in the product markets and a supplier in the resource markets.

(e) There is not enough information to tell.

13. In the simple circular-flow model which excludes the government sector, there are:

(a) Two flows—a physical flow of goods and resources and a dollar flow.

(b) Two sets of markets—product markets and resource markets.

(c) Two types of suppliers and demanders—households and business firms.

(d) Two sets of prices established—one for final goods and services and one for resources.

(e) All of the above.

14. In the circular-flow model which includes the government sector:

(a) The government buys goods and services in the product markets.

(b) The government sells goods and services in the product markets.

(c) The government provides goods and services to households and business firms directly—that is, not through the product markets.

(d) The government buys resources in the resource markets.

(e) All of the above are true.

15. The circular-flow model which includes the government sector does *not* indicate:

(a) How the government influences the level of economic activity.

(b) How the government derives its revenues.

(c) How households derive their incomes.

(d) Which sectors are buyers in the product and resource markets.

(e) Which sectors are sellers in the product and resource markets.

CHECKPOINT: LEARNING OBJECTIVES

At this point, you should be able to do all of the following:

1. Define all of the technical terms and concepts listed at the end of the chapter in the text.

2. Explain why each of the following is essential to capitalism:

(a) Private property.

(b) Self-interest and the "invisible hand."

(c) Economic individualism.

(d) Competition and free markets.

(e) The price system.

(f) Government.

3. Explain why the United States is called a "mixed economy."

4. Explain why each of the following may occur in capitalism, and discuss some economic consequences of each:

(a) Imperfect operation of the law of equal advantage.

(b) Economic inefficiency due to resource immobility, market power, and social imbalance.

(c) Inequity.

(d) Economic instability.

5. Describe the two post–World War II developments that have been particularly important in influencing the form of mixed capitalism that exists in many countries today, and discuss what mixed economies must do if they are to continue to thrive.

6. Illustrate and explain the model of the circular flow of

economic activity for an economy without a government sector, and explain why decisions regarding WHAT to produce are made in the product markets and those regarding HOW to produce are made in the resource markets.

7. Show how the introduction of a government sector changes the model above.

8. Explain why the circular-flow model:
   (a) Is a macroeconomic model.
   (b) Overlooks the problems of recession and inflation.

QUESTIONS TO THINK ABOUT

1. "People pursuing their own self-interest will achieve the best good for society only if they think and behave rationally and are motivated by economic forces." Do you agree?

2. "Laissez-faire leads to economic individualism and economic freedom. Therefore, a capitalist economy will produce maximum welfare for all people if the doctrine of complete laissez-faire is followed." Is this true?

3. "A capitalist economy must be inherently weak because producers are at the mercy of the market and cannot do what they think is best." Do you agree?

4. "If the law of equal advantage really worked, there could be no social imbalance." Is this true?

5. "If the government engaged in a massive program to eliminate income inequality today, there is no reason to believe that incomes would remain equal over time." Do you agree?

6. "Social imbalance will exist only if people do not want public goods." Is this true?

7. If social imbalance exists, it would be easier to correct the problem if the economy were operating at less than full employment than if it were fully employed. Why?

ANSWERS

Answers to Fill-in Questions

1. private
   production
   distribution
   profit
   competitive
2. private property
3. invisible hand
4. economic man
5. competition
6. many
   least
7. laissez-faire
8. price
9. mixed
10. equal advantage
11. separation of ownership and control
12. social
13. planned
14. circular flow of economic activity
15. product
    resource

Answers to True–False Questions

1. F
2. F
3. F
4. T
5. F
6. F
7. T
8. F
9. F
10. F
11. T
12. T
13. F

Answers to Multiple-Choice Questions

1. e
2. c
3. b
4. a
5. b
6. e
7. e
8. e
9. e
10. a
11. c
12. d
13. e
14. e
15. a

CHAPTER 3

The Laws of Supply and Demand: The Price System in a Pure Market Economy

CHAPTER ORIENTATION

This chapter develops and explains the following concepts:

The "law of demand," which states that there is an inverse relationship between price and the quantity demanded of a commodity.

The distinction between normal and inferior goods, and between substitute and complementary goods.

The "law of supply," which states that there is a direct relationship between price and the quantity supplied of a good.

The determination of equilibrium price and quantity in competitive markets.

Some advantages and criticisms of a pure market economy.

FILL-IN QUESTIONS

Complete the following sentences. (Answers are given at the end of the chapter.)

1. A list showing the amount of a commodity that a person would buy at different prices during a particular time interval, assuming income, tastes, and the prices of all other commodities remain the same, is called a _____ _____. A graphic representation of such a list is called a _____ _____.

2. The highest price that a person would be willing to pay to buy a certain amount of a commodity is called his _____ _____.

3. _____ states that the quantity demanded of a good varies inversely with its price, assuming that all other things which may affect demand remain the same.

4. A movement along a given demand curve is called a _____ _____

_____, whereas a shift in the demand curve due to a change in such factors as demander's income, tastes, or the price of related goods is called a _____.

5. A good for which demand varies directly with buyers' income is known as a(n) _____ good. A good for which demand varies inversely with buyers' income is known as a(n) _____ good.

6. When an increase in the price of one good leads to an increase in the demand for another, the goods are called _____. When an increase in the price of one good leads to a decrease in the demand for another, the goods are called _____.

7. A list showing the amount of a commodity that a person would sell at different prices during a particular time interval, all other things remaining the same, is called a _____. A graphic representation of such a list is called a _____.

8. The least price that is necessary to call forth a given quantity of a commodity is called the _____.

9. _____ states that the quantity supplied of a commodity usually varies directly with its price, assuming that all other factors that may determine supply remain the same.

10. A movement along a supply curve is called a _____, whereas a shift in the supply curve due to a change in such factors as resource prices or prices of related goods in production is called a _____.

11. A price at which quantity supplied equals quantity demanded is called the _____. The quantity sold at this price is called the _____.

12. When at a given market price the quantity supplied is greater than the quantity demanded, a _____ is said to exist. Conversely, when at a market price the quantity supplied is less than the quantity demanded, a _____ is said to exist.

13. When at the existing market price there is either a shortage or a surplus, the market is said to be in _____.

14. An economy in which all prices are determined by the free interplay of supply and demand is called a _____.

15. When consumers, through their dollar votes, determine indirectly what will be produced in an economy, _____ is said to exist.

PROBLEMS

(Answers are given at the end of the chapter.)

1. You are given the demand schedules of three people, Smith, Morris, and Lewis, for gin.

   (a) Calculate the total market demand.

Price per fifth	Quantity demanded by Smith	Quantity demanded by Morris	Quantity demanded by Lewis	Total market demand
$5	1	0	0	_____
4	3	2	0	_____
3	6	5	1	_____
2	10	9	4	_____
1	15	15	8	_____

   (b) In the space provided, graph each demand curve.

(c) Assume that Smith's income decreases so that at each price he is willing and able to buy 1 less fifth of gin. On your graph, show how this affects Smith's demand curve and the market demand curve. Label the new demand curves D'.

This is a change in (demand/quantity demanded) _____.

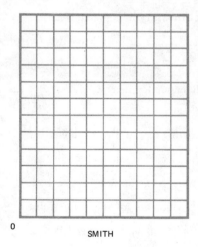

0   SMITH

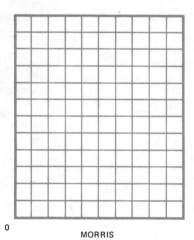

0   MORRIS

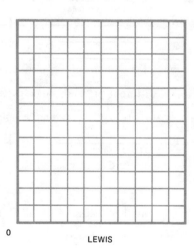

0   LEWIS

0   TOTAL MARKET

2. Below are the supply schedules of three suppliers of gin, X, Y, and Z.

(a) Calculate the total market supply schedule.

(c) Assume that resource prices increase so that at each price, each firm will supply 2 fewer units. Show this in your graph and label the new supply curves S'.

This is a change in (supply/quantity supplied)

_____.

Price	Quantity supplied by X	Quantity supplied by Y	Quantity supplied by Z	Total market supply
$5	13	10	14	_____
4	10	9	12	_____
3	5	7	9	_____
2	0	4	5	_____
1	0	0	1	_____

(b) In the space provided, graph the supply schedules.

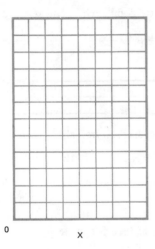

0   X

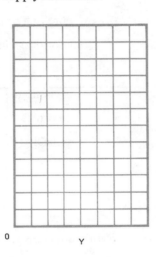

0   Y

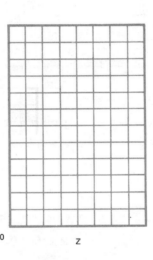

0   Z

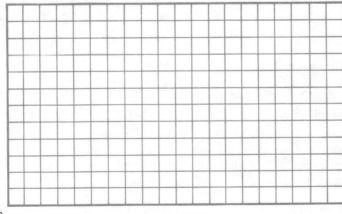

0

TOTAL MARKET

3. Shown is a graph of the supply of and demand for grass.

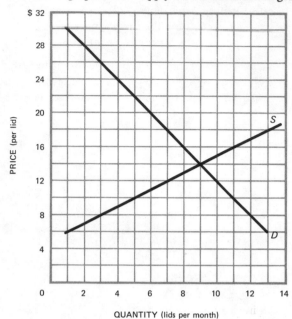

QUANTITY (lids per month)

(a) The equilibrium price is $ _____ per lid, and the equilibrium quantity is _____ lids. If the price were greater than this, there would be a (shortage/surplus) _____ of grass in the market, and competition would force the price (up/down) _____. If the price were less than this, there would be a (shortage/surplus) _____ in the market, and competition would force the price (up/down) _____ .

(b) Assume that evidence is presented which shows that grass can be injurious to health and that at every price people want to buy 3 fewer lids per month. The equilibrium price would become $ _____, and the equilibrium quantity would become _____ lids.

(c) If we assume that demand did not change but that the police increase their arrests of dealers, causing suppliers to want to sell 6 fewer lids per month at every price, then the equilibrium price would become $ _____, and the equilibrium quantity would become _____ lids.

4. Assume that the supply of and demand for beef are in equilibrium at $1.65 per pound.

(a) Assuming that beef is a normal good, an increase in income would be expected to (raise/lower/leave unchanged) _____the price of beef and (raise/lower/leave unchanged) _____ the quantity sold.

(b) This change in the price of beef (ignoring the effects of the income change itself in other markets) would tend to (raise/lower/leave unchanged) _____ the price of a substitute good such as chicken and (raise/lower/leave unchanged) _____ the quantity sold.

(c) Soybeans are high in protein and believed to be a good substitute for meat. The price of soybeans will probably (increase/decrease/remain the same) _____, and the quantity sold will probably (increase/decrease/remain the same) _____.

(d) Soybeans are used as feed for cattle. Thus, the price of beef would be likely to (increase/decrease/remain the same) _____, and the quantity sold would be likely to (increase/decrease/remain the same) _____ .

(e) Assume that the government encourages increased production of corn and other feed grains. This would tend to (raise/lower/leave unchanged) _____ _____ their prices and (raise/lower/leave unchanged) _____ the price of meat. The quantity of meat sold would probably (rise/fall/remain the same) _____.

(f) Now consumers decide to boycott meat. This would tend to _____ its price and_____ _____ the quantity sold. But if farmers held off in slaughtering, this would tend to

_____ price and _____ the

quantity sold.

SELF-TEST: TRUE–FALSE QUESTIONS

Circle T if the statement is true, F if it is false. (Answers are given at the end of the chapter.)

T F 1. If the price of beer falls and as a result people want to buy more of it, we say that demand has increased.

T F 2. If the price of beans increases, the demand for a substitute such as peas will tend to increase.

T F 3. An increase in income will increase the demand for normal goods.

T F 4. Shoes and shoelaces are complementary goods.

T F 5. If an increase in income causes the demand for potatoes to fall, potatoes are an inferior good.

T F 6. An increase in demand and a decrease in supply both cause equilibrium price to move in the same direction.

T F 7. A decrease in demand and an increase in supply both cause the equilibrium quantity to move in the same direction.

T F 8. A change in demand usually results in a change in the quantity supplied.

T F 9. A decrease in the demand price of a commodity occurs when there is a decrease in demand.

T F 10. An increase in demand causes price to rise, and this increase in price causes supply to increase.

T F 11. An increase in the price of corn will increase the quantity of corn supplied but may also decrease the supply of barley.

T F 12. Consumer sovereignty exists in a market economy only if income is more or less equally distributed.

T F 13. In a pure market economy, both technical and economic efficiency tend to be achieved.

T F 14. In a market economy, economic inequality must be the result of frictions in the market mechanism.

T F 15. If pure competition is likely to exist in any industry, it is most likely to exist in one characterized by efficient, large-scale production.

T F 16. To the extent that private and social costs diverge, or private and social benefits diverge, competitive markets will misallocate resources.

SELF-TEST: MULTIPLE-CHOICE QUESTIONS

Circle the letter that corresponds to the best answer. (Answers are given at the end of the chapter.)

1. An increase in the price of a good accompanied by a decrease in the quantity sold would result from:
   (a) An increase in demand.
   (b) A decrease in demand.
   (c) An increase in supply.
   (d) A decrease in supply.
   (e) An increase in demand accompanied by an increase in supply.

2. An increase in income will:
   (a) Increase the demand for all goods.
   (b) Increase the demand for normal goods and decrease the demand for inferior goods.
   (c) Increase the demand for normal goods and leave the demand for inferior goods unchanged.
   (d) Increase the demand for inferior goods and decrease the demand for normal goods.
   (e) Decrease the demand for inferior goods and leave the demand for normal goods unchanged.

3. Which of the following will *not* cause a change in the demand for a good?
   (a) A change in the price of substitute goods.
   (b) A change in the price of complementary goods.
   (c) A change in income.
   (d) A change in the price of the good.
   (e) A change in tastes.

4. If peas and beans are substitutes, an increase in the price of peas will:
   (a) Decrease the quantity of beans demanded.
   (b) Increase the price of beans and the quantity sold.
   (c) Increase the price of beans and decrease the quantity sold.
   (d) Increase the quantity of beans sold and leave the price of beans the same.
   (e) Not affect the market for beans.

5. If the market for cauliflower is in equilibrium and the price of fertilizer used in its cultivation rises:
   (a) The price of cauliflower will increase, and the quantity sold will decrease.
   (b) The price of cauliflower will increase, and the quantity sold will increase.
   (c) The quantity of cauliflower supplied will increase.
   (d) The supply of cauliflower will increase.
   (e) The supply of cauliflower will increase, as will the quantity of cauliflower supplied.

6. If the demand for hamburger increases:
   (a) The quantity of ketchup demanded will probably decrease.
   (b) The price of ketchup will probably rise, and the quantity sold will probably fall.
   (c) The price of ketchup will probably rise, and the quantity sold will probably rise.
   (d) The supply of hamburger will increase.
   (e) The supply of hamburger and of ketchup will probably increase.

7. If a market price is above the equilibrium price:
   (a) The price will fall, demand will increase, and supply will decrease.
   (b) The price will fall, demand will decrease, and supply will increase.
   (c) The price will fall, the quantity demanded will increase, and the quantity supplied will decrease.
   (d) The price will fall, the quantity demanded will decrease, and the quantity supplied will decrease.
   (e) Demand will decrease and supply will increase so that the market price will become an equilibrium price.

8. If we observe that over a period of time the quantity of a product sold increased and the price also increased, one possible explanation is that:
   (a) Supply increased over the period, while demand remained the same.
   (b) Supply increased over the period, while demand fell.
   (c) Demand increased over the period, while supply remained the same.
   (d) Supply decreased over the period, while demand remained the same.
   (e) Supply and demand decreased over the period.

9. Which of the following would *not* affect the supply of a commodity?
   (a) A change in its price.
   (b) A change in the price of a related good in production.
   (c) A change in resource prices.
   (d) A change in expectations about future prices.
   (e) An improvement in technology.

10. Which of the following does *not* tend to occur in a purely competitive economy?
    (a) Technical efficiency.
    (b) Income equality.
    (c) Economic growth.
    (d) Price fluctuations.
    (e) Economic efficiency.

11. A major criticism of a pure market economy is that it tends to:
    (a) Underproduce things which consumers are willing to pay for.
    (b) Overproduce goods which consumers really do not want.
    (c) Promote inefficient use of resources because producers do not know what consumers are willing to buy.
    (d) Prohibit owners of resources from using them as they wish.
    (e) Ignore or inadequately reflect all social costs and benefits associated with production and consumption.

CHECKPOINT: LEARNING OBJECTIVES

At this point, you should be able to do all of the following:

1. Define all of the technical terms and concepts listed at the end of the chapter in the text.

2. Graph demand and supply curves, given demand and supply schedules.

3. Give three reasons why the quantity demanded of a good varies inversely with its price.

4. Calculate the total market demand schedule for a product, given individuals' demand schedules.

5. Distinguish between a change in demand and a change in quantity demanded.

6. Explain why and show graphically how each of the following affects the demand for a particular product:
   (a) An increase (decrease) in buyers' money incomes.
   (b) An increase (decrease) in the price of a substitute good.
   (c) An increase (decrease) in the price of a complementary good.

7. Calculate the total market supply schedule for a good, given individual firms' supply schedules.

8. Distinguish between a change in supply and a change in quantity supplied.

9. Explain why and show graphically how each of the following affects the market supply of a particular product:
   (a) An increase (decrease) in resource prices.
   (b) An increase (decrease) in the price of related goods in production.
   (c) An increase (decrease) in the number of sellers in the market.
   (d) An improvement in technology.

10. Describe the relationship between quantity supplied and quantity demanded when the market price is:
    (a) Above equilibrium.
    (b) Below equilibrium.
    (c) At equilibrium.

11. Explain why price will tend toward its equilibrium level.

12. Explain and show graphically what happens to equilibrium price and quantity when:
    (a) Supply increases.
    (b) Supply decreases.
    (c) Demand increases.
    (d) Demand decreases.

13. Discuss the following benefits of a pure market economy:
    (a) Consumer sovereignty.
    (b) Technical and economic efficiency.
    (c) Equity.
    (d) Stability and growth.

14. Explain why a market system tends to produce income inequality.

15. Explain what happens in a market system if:
    (a) There are market imperfections and frictions.
    (b) Technology requires large-scale production.
    (c) There are social effects and externalities.

QUESTIONS TO THINK ABOUT

1. Since supply and demand are always changing, of what use is the concept "equilibrium"?

2. In periods of rapidly rising prices, government occasionally imposes price ceilings. What economic problems do price ceilings cause?

3. To control pollution, some economists have suggested that an effluent charge be imposed on polluting producers. How would this affect pollution?

4. Adam Smith tried to resolve the paradox of the price of water being very low and the price of diamonds being very high. How would you explain it?

5. When there is a housing boom, what would you expect to happen to the price of each of the following?
   (a) Lumber.
   (b) Land.
   (c) Rents on apartments.
   (d) Road-building costs.

ANSWERS

Answers to Fill-in Questions

1. demand schedule
   demand curve

2. demand price

3. The law of demand

4. change in quantity
   demanded
   change in demand

5. superior or normal
   inferior

6. substitutes
   complements

7. supply schedule
   supply curve

8. supply price

9. The law of supply

10. change in quantity
    supplied
    change in supply

11. equilibrium price
    equilibrium quantity

12. surplus
    shortage

13. disequilibrium

14. pure market economy

15. consumer sovereignty

Answers to Problems

1. (a) Total market demand

   1
   5
   12
   23
   38

   (c) demand

(b)

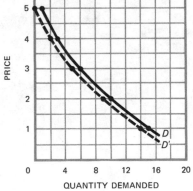

SMITH

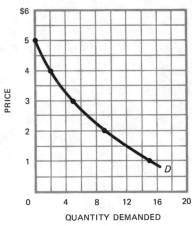

MORRIS

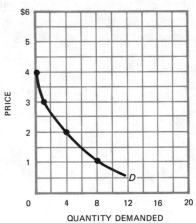

LEWIS

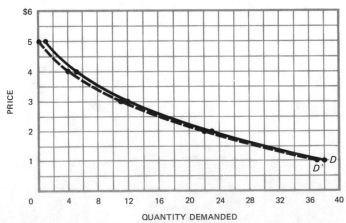

TOTAL MARKET

2. (a) Total market supply   (c) supply   3. (a) $14   (b) $12

         37   9   7

         31   surplus

         21   down   (c) $18

         9   shortage   7

         1   up

(b)

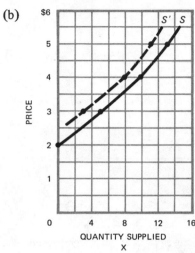 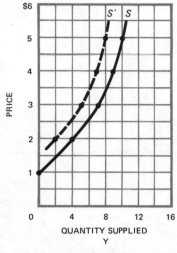 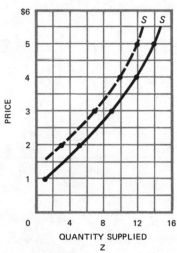

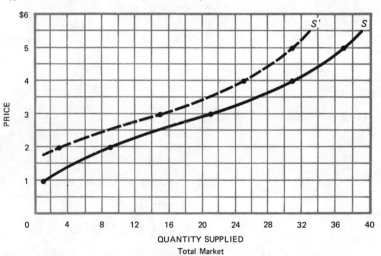

4. (a) raise   (c) increase   (e) lower   7. F   11. T   14. F

     raise   increase   lower   8. T   12. F   15. F

  (b) raise   (d) increase   rise   9. T   13. T   16. T

     raise   decrease   (f) lower   10. F

                                reduce

                                raise

                                reduce

Answers to Multiple-Choice Questions

                              1. d   5. a   9. a

                              2. b   6. c   10. b

Answers to True–False Questions   3. d   7. c   11. e

                              4. b   8. c

1. F   3. T   5. T

2. T   4. T   6. T

CHAPTER 4

Households: The Distribution of Income and Wealth

CHAPTER ORIENTATION

This chapter develops and explains the following concepts:

The definitions of and distinctions between functional income distribution and personal income distribution.

The actual distribution of income and wealth in the United States, how they have changed over the last few decades, and the factors accounting for these changes.

How the government has influenced the distribution of income and wealth.

Three criteria for the distribution of income, and the problems inherent in each.

FILL-IN QUESTIONS

Complete the following sentences. (Answers are given at the end of the chapter.)

1. The private sector of the economy consists of the _____ _____ and the _____ segment. The economy consists of both the private sector and the _____ sector.

2. The gain derived from the use of human and nonhuman resources is called _____.

3. Anything which has value because it is capable of producing income is called _____. It is a _____ of value rather than a flow.

4. Income distribution classified according to payments to owners of productive factors is called _____ _____ income distribution. It consists of _____ , _____ , _____ , and _____ .

5. Income distribution which refers to the way in which income is distributed among individuals is called _____ _____ income distribution.

6. That level of income at which half of all income recipients

receive more than this amount and half receive less is called _____ income.

7. The curve which shows the percent of income accruing to different percentiles of families is called the _____

_____

_____ .

8. The measure of income inequality which is calculated by dividing the area between the Lorenz curve and the line of income equality by the total area under the line of income equality is called the _____

_____

_____ .

9. An expenditure within or between different sectors of the economy in exchange for which no productive service is required is called a _____

_____ .

10. A tax that takes a larger percentage of the income of high-income groups than of low-income groups is called a _____ ; a tax that takes a smaller percentage of the income of high-income groups than of low-income groups is called a _____ ; and a tax that takes the same percentage of the income of all income groups is called a _____

_____ .

11. When income is distributed to people on the basis of their productive contributions, distribution is made on the basis of a(n) _____ standard; when income is distributed to people on the basis of their needs, distribution is made on the basis of a(n) _____ standard; and when income is distributed to people in such a way that each gets the same amount, distribution is made on the basis of a(n) _____ standard.

(Answers are given at the end of the chapter.)

1. Shown is a graph which is supposed to show the distribution of income in a country in a particular year as compared with what the distribution would look like if there were no income inequality.

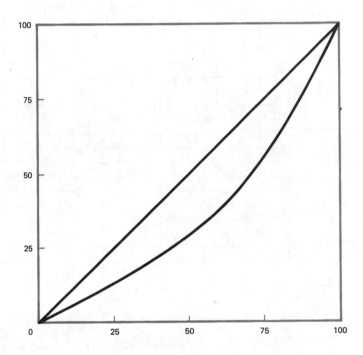

(a) Label both axes and the two curves.
(b) Shade in the area which shows the deviation of actual income distribution from a completely equal income distribution.
(c) Draw in a curve which shows income to be distributed even more unequally than it actually is.
(d) Explain what the curves bowing downward in a southeasterly direction imply about income distribution. What would it mean if the curve bowed upward in a northwesterly direction? _____

_____

_____

_____

_____

2. Draw Lorenz curves corresponding to the data given in the table. (Since you are putting two different curves on the same set of axes, make sure you label your graph correctly.)

Income rank of families	Year 2000	Year 2050
Total	100	100
Lowest fifth	6	3
Second fifth	14	7
Third fifth	15	20
Fourth fifth	25	34
Highest fifth	40	36

(a)

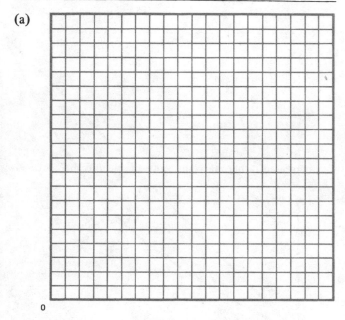

0

(b) Has income inequality increased or decreased? Discuss.

_____

_____

_____

_____

_____

_____

_____

_____

3. Draw Lorenz curves and a line showing complete equality of wealth distribution for the data given in the table. Label the graph carefully.

Wealth rank of families	Year 2000	Year 2020
Lowest fifth	1	5
Second fifth	3	10
Third fifth	8	20
Fourth fifth	20	30
Highest fifth	68	35

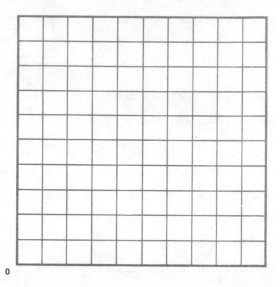

0

(a) Has wealth become more or less equally distributed?

_____

(b) Does this imply anything about what might have happened to the Lorenz curves of income distribution between the years 2000 and 2020? Discuss.

_____

_____

_____

_____

_____

_____

_____

_____

_____

_____

SELF-TEST: TRUE–FALSE QUESTIONS

Circle T if the statement is true, F if it is false. (Answers are given at the end of the chapter.)

T F 1. Income and wealth are basically the same thing.

T F 2. In our economy, the suppliers of capital receive a relatively small proportion of the total income produced in the economy.

T F 3. Because the share of total income going to rents is very small, we may conclude that landlords, as a general rule, tend to be relatively poor.

T F 4. By saying that median income has been rising in the United States, we mean that each year fewer families have less than the current median income.

T F 5. A Lorenz curve of income distribution for a country for a given year tells us nothing about the level of people's income.

T F 6. If we could redistribute wealth in this country so as to make its distribution equal among families, this would probably lead to a more equal distribution of income in the future.

T F 7. If the Gini coefficient of income inequality falls during a specified period of time, we should conclude that everybody has become richer.

T F 8. If the Gini coefficient of income inequality falls during a specified period of time, we should conclude that the actual income of the poor has increased.

T F 9. The personal distribution of income in this country has remained quite stable since 1950.

T F 10. The ratio of nonwhite to white median family income tends to rise during periods of prosperity and fall during periods when unemployment is rising.

T F 11. The concentration of wealth in our economy is more pronounced than the concentration of income.

T F 12. An increase in resource mobility would tend to reduce geographical income inequality.

T F 13. Our progressive federal income tax has been remarkably successful in reducing income inequality.

T F 14. Recipients of transfer payments are almost entirely people in the lowest income groups.

T F 15. The absolute dollar gap between the rich and the poor in the Unied States has increased despite the fact that relative shares have remained fairly stable.

T F 16. Over the long run the government has come to rely more heavily on regressive taxes.

T F 17. In the United States, income is distributed solely on the basis of the contributive standard.

SELF-TEST: MULTIPLE-CHOICE QUESTIONS

Circle the letter that corresponds to the best answer. (Answers are given at the end of the chapter.)

1. Which of the following is not a functional income share?
   (a) Wages and salaries.
   (b) Net interest.
   (c) Proprietors' income.
   (d) Corporate profits.
   (e) Social security benefits.

2. Which of the following as a percent of total income has increased rather markedly since the turn of the century?
   (a) Compensation of employees.
   (b) Corporate profits.
   (c) Proprietors' income.
   (d) Rental income.
   (e) Net interest.

3. Which of the following statements about income distribution since the mid-1950s is most accurate?
   (a) Median income of nonwhite families has fallen and that of white families has risen.
   (b) Median income of nonwhite families has remained constant and that of white families has risen.
   (c) Median income of nonwhite and of white families has risen.
   (d) Median income of nonwhite and of white families has remained virtually constant.
   (e) No data are available to determine what has happened to median income.

4. The functional distribution of income is similar to the personal distribution of income in that:
   (a) They are both solely concerned with how equitably income is distributed.
   (b) They are both primarily concerned with how equally income is distributed among families.
   (c) Neither gives any insight into how equally income is distributed.
   (d) They both show how income is distributed between the public and private sectors of the economy.
   (e) They are both concerned with "who gets what," although they consider different "whos."

5. Which of the following does *not* help explain income inequality?

(a) Inequality in the distribution of wealth.
(b) Differences in earning ability and opportunity.
(c) Differences in resource mobility.
(d) Differences in luck.
(e) They all help to explain income inequality.

6. Which of the following Gini coefficients indicates the greatest degree of income equality?
(a) 1
(b) 0.6
(c) 0.4
(d) 0.3
(e) 0.2

7. Which of the following is true of wealth?
(a) It is fairly equally distributed in this country, and this partially offsets other tendencies for income to be unequally distributed.
(b) It is fairly equally distributed, but this really does not influence income distribution.
(c) It is very unequally distributed, but this does not influence income distribution, since wealth and income are two different things.
(d) It is very unequally distributed, and this is an important cause of income inequality.
(e) It is about as equally distributed as income.

8. Which of the following probably has *not* been a major cause of the trend toward a more equal distribution of income in this country since the mid-1930s?
(a) Greater opportunities for working women and racial minority groups.
(b) The tax structure, which taxes much more from the rich than from the poor.
(c) Reductions in the low-income farm population.
(d) Larger income provisions for the unemployed.
(e) The decline of earning differentials between white-collar workers and manual workers.

9. Which of the following statements is true with regard to transfer payments?
(a) They are payments made for current contributions to production.
(b) They account for about one-half of personal income.
(c) They are all based on need.
(d) They are *not* made primarily to the lowest income groups.
(e) They have no effect on income distribution.

10. The whole system of taxes, transfers, and subsidies in the United States is:
(a) Markedly progressive.
(b) Moderately progressive or approximately proportional.

(c) Somewhat regressive.
(d) Markedly regressive.
(e) Either progressive or regressive, depending on the state of the economy.

11. Estate and gift taxes in the U.S. economy:
(a) Have markedly redistributed wealth.
(b) Have had little effect on the distribution of wealth.
(c) Have had little effect on the distribution of wealth but a marked effect on the distribution of income.
(d) Are highly progressive and without "escape clauses."
(e) Are sharply regressive.

12. In a capitalist economy, distribution is based primarily, although not exclusively, on:
(a) A contributive standard.
(b) A needs standard.
(c) An equality standard.
(d) All of the above.
(e) None of the above.

13. Which of the following statements is *false*?
(a) Unequal income distribution tends to permit a higher level of capital investment than does equal income distribution.
(b) If income is distributed on the basis of contribution to production, distribution will tend to be unequal.
(c) Distribution according to need would always produce income equality.
(d) Even if income were distributed equally, there is no reason to believe that everybody would obtain equal satisfaction.
(e) Distribution according to need must be based on nonmarket mechanisms.

CHECKPOINT: LEARNING OBJECTIVES

At this point, you should be able to do all of the following:

1. Define all of the technical terms and concepts listed at the end of the chapter in the text.

2. Describe the long-term trends in the functional distribution of income in the United States.

3. Describe the three major factors responsible for the trend in labor's share.

4. Describe what has happened to the personal distribution of income since the 1950s.

5. Explain why most of the gains in the basic income position

of nonwhites relative to whites have occurred when un-employment was low or declining.

6. Describe the distribution of wealth in the United States.

7. Construct a Lorenz curve, given data on the distribution of income or of wealth.

8. Explain how to calculate the Gini coefficient of income or wealth inequality, and explain why it must be between 0 and 1.

9. Describe what happens to a Lorenz curve if income (or wealth) becomes more equally or less equally distributed.

10. Give four important reasons for income inequality.

11. Explain why the Gini coefficient of income inequality has been declining gradually in the United States since the 1930s.

12. Describe the three sets of measures used by the government to alter the distribution of income, and the impact which each has had on distribution.

13. Describe the degree to which the overall tax system has affected income distribution.

14. Describe the types of taxes that the government uses to alter the distribution of wealth, and state how effective they have been in doing so.

15. Explain why income in the United States is said to be distributed primarily on the basis of a contributive standard.

16. Explain the problems that would arise in trying to distribute income on the basis of needs.

17. Explain why equal income distribution is not necessarily

"just," and is likely to result in declining economic progress.

QUESTIONS TO THINK ABOUT

1. Why would economists be interested in both functional and personal income distribution? Wouldn't one type of distribution give them all the information they need?

2. "The only difference between wealth and income is the time period they cover. Income tells us how much we are earning today, whereas wealth tells us how much we earned in the past." Is this true?

3. If wealth were redistributed equally to all people, is there any reason to believe that it would remain equally distributed over time?

4. Does a Gini coefficient of inequality imply anything about equity? Why or why not?

5. Would a job information service that described jobs available all over the country be likely to influence income distribution? How?

6. "The criterion of 'equity' could be used to justify income distribution based on merit, on need, and on equality." Do you agree?

7. "The only equitable transfer payments are those that distribute income to the poor." Do you agree?

8. "Since needs are largely nonmeasurable, and income equality does not ensure equality of satisfaction, the only reasonable method of distribution is that based solely on contribution to production." Do you agree?

Answers to Fill-in Questions

1. household
   business
   public

2. income

3. wealth
   stock

4. functional
   wages
   rent
   interest
   profit

5. personal

6. median

7. Lorenz curve of income
   distribution

8. Gini coefficient of income
   inequality

9. transfer payment

10. progressive tax
    regressive tax
    proportional tax

11. contributive
    needs
    equality

Answers to Problems

1. (a), (b), (c)

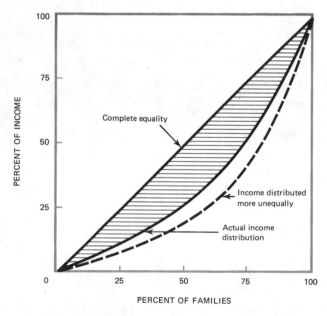

(d) Bowing down simply implies that income is distributed unequally. The curve cannot bow upward—it would make no sense. It would imply, for example, that the *lowest* fifth of families got *more* than one-fifth of total income.

2. (a)

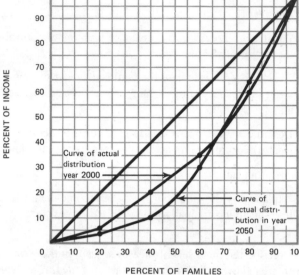

(b) The poor have become relatively poorer, but the rich have become relatively poorer also. Middle-income people, on the other hand, have become relatively richer. But the Gini coefficient for the year 2050 is larger than for the year 2000. (It is apparent that the area between the line of complete income equality and the curve of actual distribution in 2050 is larger than the area between the line of complete income equality and the curve of actual distribution in 2000. Since the triangular area is the same for both years, it follows that the Gini coefficient for year 2050 is larger than the Gini coefficient for 2000.) Therefore, income inequality increased between 2000 and 2050.

3.

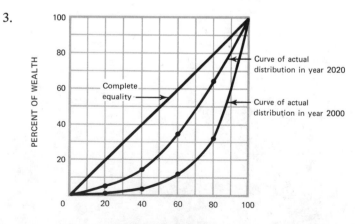

(a) more equally distributed

(b) Since income derives in part from wealth, more equal distribution of wealth might result in more equal distribution of income. Whether income becomes more equally distributed or not depends also on what happens to the distribution of income that derives from factors other than wealth. If these other factors leave distribution roughly unchanged, then the more equal distribution of wealth would have the effect of putting the Lorenz curve of income distribution in 2020 closer to the line of perfect income equality than the Lorenz curve of income distribution in 2000.

Answers to True–False Questions

1.	F	3.	F	5.	T
2.	T	4.	F	6.	T

7.	F	11.	T	15.	T
8.	F	12.	T	16.	T
9.	T	13.	F	17.	F
10.	T	14.	F		

Answers to Multiple-Choice Questions

1.	e	6.	e	10.	b
2.	a	7.	d	11.	b
3.	c	8.	b	12.	a
4.	e	9.	d	13.	c
5.	e				

CHAPTER 5

Insecurity and America's Poor: Can Poverty Be Eliminated?

CHAPTER ORIENTATION

This chapter develops and explains the following concepts:

The nature of our present social security system, and some problems with regard to its financing.

Poverty and some of its causes.

Family allowances, guaranteed annual incomes, negative income taxes, and an income allowance plan, all of which are means of alleviating poverty.

Minimum-wage legislation and manpower programs, which are attempts to attack poverty through the labor market.

FILL-IN QUESTIONS

Complete the following sentences. (Answers are given at the end of the chapter.)

1. The _____ Act of 1935 provides for both social insurance programs and a public charity program. Under one of the social insurance programs, _____

    _____ are paid for a specified number of weeks to covered workers who are involuntarily unemployed.

2. The _____ is a sliding income scale which attempts to measure the level of income below which people have a completely inadequate standard of living.

3. Under a _____

    _____, every family in the country would receive a certain amount of money from the government based exclusively on the number and age of its children. Under a _____

    _____, only families below the poverty line would receive money, the amount depending on family size and income.

4. A _____
is a type of reverse income tax under which poor people
would receive enough money from the government to
either reduce or close the gap between what they earned
and some explicit minimum income level.

5. The _____

_____

is the basic minimum-wage law in the United States.

6. _____

are deliberate efforts undertaken in the private and public
sectors to develop and use the capacities of people who are
actual or potential members of the labor force.

7. A labor market which, in effect, consists of two separate
markets, one having relatively good wages and working
conditions and the other having relatively poor wages and
working conditions, is called a _____

_____ .

PROBLEMS

(Answers are given at the end of the chapter.)

1. Assume that to help alleviate poverty the government
passed a negative income tax which paid each household
consisting of four people on the basis of the following
formula:

Government payment = $3,000 − (0.4 × earned income)

(a) The most that the government would pay such a
household is $ _____ .

(b) A family will receive no payment from the government
when its income is $_____ and above.

(c) If the poverty line for a family of four is $4,000, the
family must earn $ _____ to obtain this much
income in total.

2. Assume that the government granted each person an
allowance of $1,000 and imposed a flat-rate 40 percent tax
on earned income.

(a) The least amount of total income that a family of
four could have is $ _____ .

(b) If a family of four has earned income of $8,000, its
disposable income will be $ _____ .

(c) When the earned income of a family of four reaches
$ _____ , its disposable income will equal its
earned income. At any level of earned income greater
than this, its disposable income will be (more than/
equal to/less than) _____ its
earned income.

(d) If the poverty line for a family of four is $5,000, in
order for a family of four to receive at least this much
income, its earned income must be at least $ _____ .

3. The following diagram shows the supply of and demand for
unskilled labor in a competitive labor market.

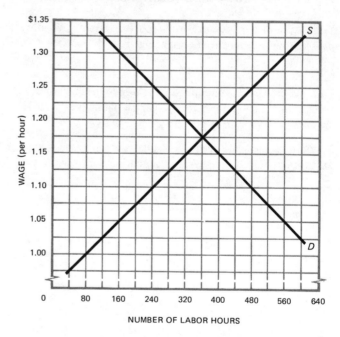

(a) In the absence of a minimum wage, _____ people
will be employed, assuming that each works an 8-hour
day. The wage will be $ _____ per hour.

(b) Assume that a minimum wage of $1.25 per hour is
imposed. _____ people will be employed, assuming

that each works an 8-hour day, and _____ people who were previously working will become unemployed.

(c) Imposition of a minimum wage (in this case) has (increased/left unchanged/decreased) _____ the total income of this group of workers. Has the minimum wage helped alleviate poverty? _____

_____

_____

_____

_____

_____

SELF-TEST: TRUE–FALSE QUESTIONS

Circle T if the statement is true, F if it is false. (Answers are given at the end of the chapter.)

T F 1. The OASDHI program is basically a form of public welfare in that every citizen, by law, is entitled to benefits when they become old, disabled, etc.

T F 2. Unemployment benefits discourage work effort because once a person has worked, he can keep drawing benefits as long as he is unemployed.

T F 3. General assistance programs are financed and administered by all levels of government, not just the federal government.

T F 4. The social security tax is, in fact, regressive.

T F 5. People in the United States who are "poor" do not, in general, own durable goods such as refrigerators, cars, and television sets.

T F 6. Most poor Americans are white.

T F 7. The basic difference between a family allowance plan and a guaranteed annual income is that the latter assures all people an income above the poverty line, whereas the former does not.

T F 8. A major problem with a guaranteed annual

income is that people are as well off financially if they do not work as they would be if they did work.

T F 9. A negative income tax would guarantee that a family that earned some income would receive more money in total than a comparable family that earned no income.

T F 10. A negative income tax would provide coverage to more poor families than the current welfare programs do.

T F 11. When a minimum wage above the existing wage is established in a competitive labor market, some people are likely to become unemployed.

T F 12. Proponents of minimum-wage legislation argue that minimum wages encourage efficiency in the use of resources.

T F 13. Minimum wages are, in general, an effective means of reducing poverty.

T F 14. Poverty would be greatly reduced if the secondary labor market were outlawed.

SELF-TEST: MULTIPLE-CHOICE QUESTIONS

Circle the letter that corresponds to the best answer. (Answers are given at the end of the chapter.)

1. Which of the following is *not* specifically covered under U.S. social insurance programs?
   (a) Unemployment.
   (b) Total disability.
   (c) Old age.
   (d) Poverty.
   (e) Health needs of the elderly.

2. Which of the following is *not* a criticism of the current social security system?
   (a) Only people who have contributed to the fund can receive such benefits as housing subsidies and medical assistance.
   (b) Contributions are compulsory, so people cannot select and pay for the particular benefits they want.
   (c) Financing is regressive, so low- and middle-income families bear the greatest burden of the tax.
   (d) The payroll tax tends to have a destabilizing effect on the economy.
   (e) There is a disparity between benefits received by families from the program and their payments into it.

3. Which of the following would *not* make financing of the social security program more progressive?
   (a) Revising the payroll tax to permit a certain amount of income to be exempt from taxation.
   (b) Replacing the payroll tax by the income tax.
   (c) Financing the program out of general federal tax revenues.
   (d) Replacing the payroll tax by a fixed tax on income up to a specified minimum income level.
   (e) All of the above would make financing more progressive.

4. Under a negative income tax where government payments = $3,000 - \frac{1}{2} \times$ earned income, the break-even level of income would be:
   (a) $1,500.
   (b) $3,000.
   (c) $4,500.
   (d) $5,200.
   (e) $6,000.

5. If the government gave an income allowance of $3,000 to a family of four and imposed a 25 percent tax on earned income, the family's disposable income would be greater than its earned income if its earned income was:
   (a) Less than $15,000.
   (b) Greater than $12,000.
   (c) Less than $12,000.
   (d) Between $3,000 and $15,000.
   (e) Between $4,000 and $13,000.

6. A negative income tax and an income allowance plan both include:
   (a) A minimum level of income which would be received by everybody.
   (b) A provision for relating government payments to the level of income.
   (c) A break-even level of income at which the government payment is zero.
   (d) All of the above.
   (e) None of the above.

7. Which of the following is *not* a major advantage to a negative income tax?
   (a) There would be no need to establish a new government agency to administer it.
   (b) Administrative costs would be negligible.
   (c) Income deficiency would be the only criterion for establishing eligibility for subsidy.
   (d) The incentive to work in order to gain more income would not be reduced.
   (e) All of the above are major advantages.

8. An increase in the minimum wage would probably:
   (a) Increase the wages of all workers.
   (b) Increase employment in low-wage industries as more workers became attracted to them.
   (c) Eliminate poverty.
   (d) Eliminate the secondary labor market by raising the wages that employers must pay.
   (e) Reduce exploitation in monopsonistic labor markets.

9. Evidence suggests that statutory minimum wages have, in fact:
   (a) Reduced poverty markedly.
   (b) Increased employment prospects for the disadvantaged.
   (c) Eliminated the causes of poverty.
   (d) Created unemployment among certain classes of labor.
   (e) Eliminated the need for manpower programs.

CHECKPOINT: LEARNING OBJECTIVES

At this point you should be able to do all of the following:

1. Define all of the technical terms and concepts listed at the end of the chapter in the text.

2. Describe the major provisions of the Social Security Act of 1935.

3. Give three reasons why Social Security is not, in a meaningful sense, an insurance program.

4. Describe some ways in which financing of the social security system could be made more equitable.

5. Distinguish between the following types of poverty:
   (a) Cyclical.
   (b) Community.
   (c) Personal.

6. Explain the difference between a family-allowance system and a guaranteed annual income.

7. Describe and illustrate numerically how a negative income tax would work, and state its primary advantages and disadvantages.

8. Describe and illustrate numerically how an income allowance plan would work.

9. State the three variables that all income plans in existence or under serious discussion have in common.

10. Show graphically the effects of a statutory minimum wage in a competitive labor market.

11. State the arguments both for and against minimum wages.

12. State what, in fact, minimum wages appear to have accomplished for the poor.

13. State what manpower policies must do in a dual labor market to eliminate the causes of poverty.

QUESTIONS TO THINK ABOUT

1. If, in fact, a dual labor market exists, does it make any sense to require welfare recipients to receive job training and to then seek employment?

2. A large fraction of welfare families have minor children and unskilled female heads of household. Describe a comprehensive program that might help such families break out of the poverty cycle.

3. The federal government pays a large part of welfare costs on a contributory basis with the states. Some states have been much more generous than others in providing benefits. What are some difficulties that this nonuniformity of benefits is likely to cause? Should individuals in some states have to bear a higher burden of welfare costs than individuals in others? Should financing be put purely on a federal basis?

4. Welfare costs have skyrocketed in recent years, yet payments to families are pitifully low. What might have caused this? Is there any solution?

5. Given the enormous costs of welfare, why is there so much opposition to other types of income-maintenance programs?

6. Assume that you are an adviser to a state that is setting up some manpower programs. What types of programs would you suggest? How should they be financed? How can you be sure that people who have undergone training will be able to get and hold jobs?

7. The women's liberation movement has pushed for, and in many cases received, wage increases for women so that they are making salaries equivalent to those received by men in equivalent jobs. Is this likely to affect the employment of women? The number of women in the labor market?

ANSWERS

Answers to Fill-in Questions

1. Social Security unemployment benefits

2. poverty line

3. family allowance plan guaranteed annual income

4. negative income tax

5. Fair Labor Standards Act of 1938

6. Manpower policies

7. dual labor market

Answers to Problems

1. (a) $3,000
    (b) $7,500
    (c) $1,667 [Its earned income (EI) plus its government payment ($3,000 − 0.4EI$) must equal $4,000. Thus,

$$EI + (\$3,000 - 0.4EI) = \$4,000$$
$$0.6EI = \$1,000$$
$$EI = \$1,667.]$$

2. (a) $4,000
    (b) $8,800
    (c) $10,000 [Its disposable income (DI) equals EI + $4,000 − 0.4EI$, or $4,000 + 0.6EI$. If $DI = EI$, then $DI = EI = \$4,000 + 0.6EI$ or $EI = \$10,000.$]
    less than
    (d) $1,667

3. (a) 45
    $1.175

(b) 30
    15
(c) decreased
    It has helped those who remain employed but hurt those who have lost their jobs. Since total income has fallen, the law has probably done more harm than good.

Answers to True–False Questions

1.	F	8.	F
2.	F	9.	T
3.	T	10.	T
4.	T	11.	T
5.	F	12.	T
6.	T	13.	F
7.	F (Either plan could, but need not, provide this assurance.)	14.	F

Answers to Multiple-Choice Questions

1.	d	6.	d
2.	a	7.	b
3.	d	8.	e
4.	e	9.	d
5.	c		

CHAPTER 6

Government: Functions, Social Goods, and Taxation

CHAPTER ORIENTATION

This chapter develops and explains the following concepts:

The economic scope and functions of the government sector.

The nature of "spillovers," how they affect the free-market allocation of resources, and some things that the government can do to reduce them or to offset their effects.

Budgeting, and the different sources of revenue for and types of expenditures made by each level of government.

The benefit and ability-to-pay principles of taxation.

The distinctions between proportional, progressive, and regressive taxes, and between direct and indirect taxes.

FILL-IN QUESTIONS

Complete the following sentences. (Answers are given at the end of the chapter.)

1. When the benefits of a good accrue only to those who pay for it, the good is subject to the _____ principle.

2. External benefits or costs that result from activities for which no compensation is made are called _____ _____ .

3. Goods whose benefits are indivisible so that no one can be excluded from receiving them, whether he pays for them or not, are called _____ .

4. A payment (usually by government) to households or businesses that enables them to consume or produce a product in larger quantities or at lower prices than they would otherwise is called a _____ . When it is a fixed amount per unit of the product bought or produced, it is called a _____ _____ .

5. An itemized estimate of expected revenues and expenditures for a given period in the future is called a _____ _____ .

6. Revenues received by one level of government from another are called _____.

7. The total personal income tax as a percent of total taxable income is called the _____ tax rate. The change in the total personal income tax as a percent of change in total taxable income is called the _____ tax rate.

8. _____ equity refers to the idea that "equals should be treated equally," whereas _____ equity refers to the idea that "unequals should be treated unequally."

9. The _____ principle holds that people should be taxed according to the benefits they derive from public services, whereas the _____ _____ principle holds that people should be taxed according to their income or wealth.

10. To calculate the amount of a tax that must be paid on something, we multiply the value of the object being taxed, called the _____, by the percentage of the value of the object that must be paid to the government, which is called the _____.

11. A tax that takes the same percentage of income from high-income taxpayers as from low-income taxpayers is called a _____ tax; a tax that takes a larger percentage of income from high-income taxpayers than from low-income taxpayers is called a _____ tax; and a tax that takes a smaller percentage of income from high-income taxpayers than from low-income taxpayers is called a _____ tax.

12. When the burden of a tax is not borne by the person or firm on whom the tax is imposed, the tax is said to be _____.

13. Taxes whose burdens are borne by the persons or firms on whom they are imposed are called _____ taxes; those whose burdens are not borne or only partly borne by the persons or firms on whom they are imposed are called _____ taxes.

PROBLEMS

(Answers are given at the end of the chapter.)

1. The supply and demand curves, S and D, shown in the figure, reflect only private benefits and costs.

(a) The equilibrium price is $_____, and the equilibrium quantity is _____ units.

(b) Assume that the production of the good results in spillover costs of $4 per unit. The socially optimal output then is _____ units. Thus, from society's point of view, the firm is producing (too much/too little/there is not enough information to tell) _____ of the good.

(c) To encourage producers to produce the socially optimal output, the government could impose a specific (tax/subsidy) _____ of $ _____ per unit on producers.

(d) Now, if the production of the product did not involve spillover costs but instead yielded $2 per unit of spillover benefits, the socially optimal output would be _____ units. Thus, from society's point of view, the firm is producing (too much/too little/there is not enough information to tell) _____ _____ of the good.

(e) To encourage producers to produce the socially optimal output, the government could impose a specific (tax/subsidy) _____ on producers of $ _____ per unit.

2. Given the following information, calculate the average tax rate at different levels of income and the marginal tax rate as incomes rise.

Total taxable income	Total personal income tax	Average tax rate (%)	Marginal tax rate (%)
$ 1,000	$ 0	_____	
2,000	180	_____	_____
3,000	350	_____	_____
4,000	500	_____	_____
5,000	630	_____	_____
10,000	1,130	_____	_____
20,000	1,930	_____	_____

(a) Is this tax regressive, proportional, or progressive? Explain. _____
_____
_____
_____
_____
_____

SELF-TEST: TRUE–FALSE QUESTIONS

Circle T if the statement if true, F if it is false. (Answers are given at the end of the chapter.)

T F 1. The network of government tariffs, price supports, and quotas often results in the misallocation of resources.

T F 2. Cable television is a good example of a public good.

T F 3. Any good whose marginal cost is zero and whose production or consumption involves spillovers is a public good.

T F 4. If the production of a good involves spillover costs, the free-market price will be higher than it would be if there were no spillover costs.

T F 5. Specific subsidies can offset the tendency for producers to underallocate resources to goods which have spillover benefits.

T F 6. If the government offsets the damage to the environment caused by polluting firms, the free market cannot be accused of misallocating resources.

T F 7. Historically, the single most important cause of the increase in federal government spending has been wars and national defense.

T F 8. Since wages of public employees have not risen along with wages of private employees, and increases in productivity in the production of public services have been much greater than increases in productivity in the private sector, there has been a decrease in the costs of the government's provision of civilian benefits.

T F 9. The largest single use of federal revenue is education.

T F 10. The largest single source of state and local government revenue is the property tax.

T F 11. The largest single use of state and local government revenue is welfare payments.

T F 12. Over the long run, the proportion of total tax revenues going to state and local governments has been increasing, and that going to the federal government has been decreasing.

T F 13. When a particular tax has the characteristic that the average tax rate increases with income, that tax is progressive.

T F 14. With increasing marginal income tax rates, a person might find that he could not afford to work overtime because, if he did, his after-tax income would fall.

T F 15. Although the structure of the property tax is proportional, on an income base it tends to be regressive.

T F 16. A value-added tax on all items tends to be progressive.

T F 17. The sales tax unquestionably reflects the ability-to-pay principle, in that the higher your income, the more you purchase, and the larger is your tax burden.

T F 18. Whereas the social security tax paid by an employer is indirect, the social security tax paid by an employee is direct.

SELF-TEST: MULTIPLE-CHOICE QUESTIONS

Circle the letter that corresponds to the best answer. (Answers are given at the end of the chapter.)

1. Which of the following comes closest to being a public good?
   (a) Railroads.
   (b) Toll highways.
   (c) Air traffic control.
   (d) Public utilities.
   (e) Bus services.

2. Which of the following is characteristic of public goods but of no other type of goods?
   (a) They are not subject to the exclusion principle.
   (b) They are not sold in the private market.
   (c) The cost of providing them to one more user is negligible.
   (d) They are produced by government.
   (e) They involve spillovers.

3. Goods that have spillover costs but no spillover benefits tend to be:
   (a) Overproduced by the private sector.
   (b) Underproduced by the private sector.
   (c) Optimally produced by the private sector.
   (d) Sometimes over- and sometimes underproduced by the private sector.
   (e) Rarely produced by the private sector.

4. To promote the optimal allocation of resources to goods that yield spillover benefits, the government could:
   (a) Tax producers.
   (b) Prohibit the production of such goods.
   (c) Insist that producers raise their prices.
   (d) Subsidize producers.
   (e) Limit the amount of such goods that people may buy.

5. Which of the following has *not* been a cause of the rise in total government expenditures in our economy?

   (a) Increased defense costs.
   (b) Inflation.
   (c) Lagging productivity in the government sector.
   (d) Increased demand for public goods.
   (e) All of the above have caused total government expenditures to rise.

6. Which of the following types of tax is progressive on an income basis?
   (a) A sales tax.
   (b) A property tax.
   (c) The federal income tax.
   (d) Any direct tax.
   (e) An excise tax.

7. The VAT:
   (a) Is a major source of revenue in the United States.
   (b) Has a relatively narrow base.
   (c) Would be regressive if applied to all goods.
   (d) Would discourage expenditures on new plant and equipment.
   (e) Would be very helpful in stabilizing the economy.

8. Which of the following taxes is based on the benefit principle?
   (a) The personal income tax.
   (b) A sales tax.
   (c) A gift tax.
   (d) A corporation income tax.
   (e) A gasoline tax.

9. One problem with the benefit principle of taxation is that:
   (a) It has a narrow base.
   (b) Nobody benefits from having to pay taxes.
   (c) It is difficult to determine how the benefits of public services are distributed.
   (d) It tends to require very high tax rates.
   (e) Only the poor would be taxed since only they receive the benefits of public services.

10. Which of the following is an example of a direct tax?
    (a) The property tax on rental units.
    (b) A sales tax.
    (c) A social security tax paid by employers.
    (d) Estate and inheritance taxes.
    (e) An excise tax.

11. If a $1 per unit tax is imposed on a producer and this causes his price to increase by $.40, then the tax must be:
    (a) Proportional.
    (b) Progressive.
    (c) Regressive.
    (d) Direct.
    (e) Indirect.

CHECKPOINT: LEARNING OBJECTIVES

At this point, you should be able to do all of the following:

1. Define all of the technical terms and concepts listed at the end of the chapter in the text.

2. Discuss the six ways in which the government promotes and regulates the private sector.

3. State the three characteristics of public goods, and explain whether or not a public good *must* have all of these characteristics.

4. Explain and show graphically why the competitive market tends to underallocate resources to the production of goods that have spillover benefits and overallocate resources to the production of goods that have spillover costs.

5. Explain how each of the following government actions could either eliminate or offset the effects of spillovers:
   (a) Regulation.
   (b) Imposition of specific taxes and/or specific subsidies.
   (c) Mitigation.

6. State two major causes of the steep increases in government spending which have occurred over the past few decades.

7. Describe the major sources of revenue to and types of expenditures by:
   (a) The federal government.
   (b) State and local governments.

8. Describe the primary purpose of intergovernmental grants-in-aid.

9. Describe the taxes that exist in the United States which are based on:
   (a) Income.
   (b) Wealth.
   (c) Activities.

10. Distinguish between marginal and average tax rates.

11. Distinguish between progressive, proportional, and regressive taxes, and give some examples of each.

12. Explain each of the following criteria for judging the relative merits of a tax:
    (a) Equity.
    (b) Efficiency.
    (c) Enforceability.

13. Explain the benefit and ability-to-pay principles of tax equity, and discuss some problems inherent in each.

14. Distinguish between direct and indirect taxes, and give some examples of each.

15. Explain why there may be increased reliance in the United States on indirect as opposed to direct taxes in the future.

QUESTIONS TO THINK ABOUT

1. "When a good involves spillover benefits, the subsidizing of producers merely shifts these benefits to the producers and accomplishes little else." Do you agree?

2. "All goods involve spillovers. Therefore, it makes no sense to distinguish public from private goods." Is this true?

3. Some argue that our overall tax system is becoming less equitable. Do you agree?

4. "Revenue sharing," in which the federal government shares its revenues with the states, is a much debated issue. What would be some advantages of revenue sharing? Can you see any disadvantages?

5. The government provides many goods which are not public goods. Can you give some examples and explain why the government might be providing them?

ANSWERS

Answers to Fill-in Questions

1. exclusion
2. spillovers
3. public goods
4. subsidy
   specific subsidy
5. budget
6. grants-in-aid
7. average
   marginal
8. Horizontal
   vertical
9. benefit
   ability-to-pay
10. tax base
    tax rate
11. proportional
    progressive
    regressive
12. shifted
13. direct
    indirect

Answers to Problems

1. (a) $8
       9
   (b) 7
       too much
   (c) tax
       $4
   (d) 10
       too little
   (e) subsidy
       $2

2.

Average tax rate (%)	Marginal tax rate (%)
0	
	18
9	
	17
11.7	
	15
12.5	
	13
12.6	
	10
11.3	
	8
9.6	

(a) The tax is progressive up to an income of $5,000, because to this level of income the average tax rate is rising. But when income is $10,000 and above, the average tax rate declines, indicating that the tax becomes regressive. There is not enough information to determine at what level of income between $5,000 and $10,000 the tax becomes regressive.

Answers to True-False Questions

1. T
2. F
3. F
4. F
5. T
6. F
7. T
8. F
9. F
10. T
11. F
12. T
13. T
14. F (This assumes, of course, that marginal tax rates do not rise over 100 percent.)
15. T
16. F
17. F
18. T

Answers to Multiple-Choice Questions

1. c
2. a
3. a
4. d
5. e
6. c
7. c
8. e
9. c
10. d
11. e

PART 2

National Income, Employment, and Fiscal Policy

CHAPTER 7

National Income and Product: How Do We Measure the Economy's Performance?

CHAPTER ORIENTATION

This chapter develops and explains the following concepts:

The definition of the most comprehensive measure of a nation's economic activity — its gross national product (GNP).

The calculation of GNP from the point of view of both expenditures and income.

How GNP estimates for a series of years can be adjusted so as to reveal the changes in real output that have occurred over time.

Some reasons why GNP is an imperfect indicator of changes in society's well-being over time.

Net national product (NNP), national income (*NI*), personal income (*PI*), and disposable personal income (*DPI*), which are other measures of income and output.

FILL-IN QUESTIONS

Complete the following sentences. (Answers are given at the end of the chapter.)

1. The total market value of all final goods and services produced by an economy during a year is called the

   _____.

2. An expenditure within or between different sectors of the economy in exchange for which no productive service is required is called a _____

   _____.

3. Additions to or replacement of real productive assets is called _____.

4. Stocks of goods that business firms have on hand, including raw materials, supplies, and finished goods, are called

   _____.

5. When gross investment is less than depreciation, we say that _____ occurs.

6. The decline in the value of existing physical capital due to wear and tear, obsolescence, destruction, and accidental loss is called _____

   _____

and consists primarily of _____ of business plant and equipment and owner-occupied houses.

7. The sum of payments made to the owners of the factors of production for services rendered by those factors is called _____ .

8. The total market value of goods and services available to a society for either consumption or additions to its stock of capital is called _____ _____ .

9. The total income people receive from all sources is called _____ _____ .

10. The income received by people from all sources which is actually available for spending is called _____ _____ .

11. The sum of wages, rent, interest, profit, indirect business taxes, and depreciation contributed at any stage in the production of a good is called the _____ _____ at that stage of production.

12. By _____ output we mean output measured in such a way that its value is unaffected by price changes.

13. When GNP in any year is expressed in terms of the actual prices that existed during that year, GNP is said to be expressed in _____ dollars. But when calculated in terms of the actual prices of some previous year, GNP is said to be expressed in _____ _____ dollars.

14. When a series of current dollar values is divided by a price index, the current values are said to be _____ _____ .

15. The total amount spent on the nation's output of final goods and services by the four sectors of the economy is called _____ _____ .

PROBLEMS

(Answers are given at the end of the chapter.)

1. You are given the following information about output and prices for three different years.

Year	Number of units of output	Price per unit of output in current dollars	Value of output in current dollars
1	5	3	_____
2	7	2	_____
3	6	4	_____

(a) Fill in the value of output in current dollars. The highest current dollar output occurred in Year _____ .

(b) Using the information above, calculate the following:

Year t	Price in Year t as a % of price in Year 1	Price in Year t as a % of price in Year 2	Price in Year t as a % of price in Year 3
1	_____	_____	_____
2	_____	_____	_____
3	_____	_____	_____

(c) Using the information you now have, fill in the following table:

Year	Value of output in constant dollars of Year 1	Value of output in constant dollars of Year 2	Value of output in constant dollars of Year 3
1	_____	_____	_____
2	_____	_____	_____
3	_____	_____	_____

(d) In constant dollars of Year 1, GNP of Year _____ is largest, GNP of Year _____ is next largest, and GNP of Year _____ is smallest. In constant dollars of Year 2, GNP of Year _____ is largest, GNP of Year _____ is next largest, and GNP of Year _____ is smallest. And in constant dollars of Year 3, GNP of Year _____ is largest, GNP of Year _____ is next largest, and GNP of Year _____ is smallest.

(e) What conclusion can you derive from the results you obtained in part (d)? _____ _____ _____

_____

_____

_____

_____

_____

_____

(f)   Now calculate:

Value of GNP in Year 1 in dollars of Year 1 as a % of:	Value of GNP in Year 1 in dollars of Year 2 as a % of:	Value of GNP in Year 1 in dollars of Year 3 as a % of:
Value of GNP in Year 2 in dollars of Year 1 _____	Value of GNP in Year 2 in dollars of Year 2 _____	Value of GNP in Year 2 in dollars of Year 3 _____
Value of GNP in Year 3 in dollars of Year 1 _____	Value of GNP in Year 3 in dollars of Year 2 _____	Value of GNP in Year 3 in dollars of Year 3 _____

(g)   What conclusions can you draw from the results you

obtained in part (f)? _____

_____

_____

_____

2. (Questions 2–6 must be done sequentially, as they are all
part of the same problem.) Consider an economy whose
only products are $10 of fertilizer, $70 of apples, and $30
of cider. Some apples are used for final consumption, and
those which are not are used to produce cider. Each
industry consists of only one firm. None of the firms
experience depreciation or pay indirect business taxes.
Their income statements are as follows:

Fertilizer firm		Apple firm		Cider firm	
Value of fertilizer produced	$10	Value of apples produced	$70	Value of cider produced	$30
Wages	2	Fertilizer	10	Apples	10
Rent	4	Wages	20	Wages	2
Interest	3	Rent	5	Rent	3
Profit	_____	Interest	30	Interest	5
		Profit	_____	Profit	_____

(a)   Calculate the profit for each firm, and fill in the appropriate blanks in the income statements above.

(b) To calculate GNP from the expenditures viewpoint, we
would add $ _____ of fertilizer, $ _____ of apples,
and $ _____ of cider. GNP is $ _____.

(c) To calculate GNP from the income viewpoint, we
would add the items _____ ,

_____ , _____ , and

_____ at all stages of production. Doing

this, we find that GNP is $ _____.

3. Consider a firm producing apples that uses no intermediate
products and pays no indirect business taxes but does use
capital equipment which depreciates in the production
process. Its income statement is as follows:

Value of apples produced	$100
Wages	30
Rent	20
Interest	15
Depreciation	10
Profit	_____

(a) Calculate the firm's profit, and enter it in the income
statement.

(b) If apples are all final products, the contribution of this
firm to the GNP by the product viewpoint is $ _____.

(c) From part (b) we see that the sum of wages, rent,
interest, and profit does not equal the value of the
product produced by a firm if it experiences _____
_____ of its capital
stock. Since this enters as a _____ of
production and contributes to the value of product
produced (this firm's contribution to the GNP), in
order to calculate its contribution to the GNP from
the earnings viewpoint we must add not only _____
_____ , _____ , _____
_____ , and _____ ,
but also _____ . To calculate
GNP for the economy we must therefore add these
things for _____ firms in _____ stages of
production.

4. Now consider a firm which produces peas. Assume that is uses no intermediate products or capital equipment but does pay indirect business taxes in the form of a property tax. Its income statement is as follows:

Value of peas produced	$200
Wages	75
Rent	40
Interest	20
Property tax	10
Profit	_____

(a) Calculate the firm's profit and enter it in the income statement.

(b) If all of the peas are final product, this firm's contribution to the GNP from the product viewpoint is $ _____ .

(c) Again we see that the sum of wages, rent, interest, and profit does not necessarily equal the value of product produced. In this case it does not, because the firm pays _____

_____ .

Since this is a _____ of production and contributes to the value of the product produced, to calculate this firm's contribution to the GNP from the earnings viewpoint we must add not only _____

_____ , _____ ,

_____ , and _____ but

also _____

_____ . To calculate GNP for the economy we must therefore add these things for _____ firms in _____ stages of production.

5. Now let us consider the implications of Problems 2, 3, and 4. In our economy, firms typically do use intermediate products, do experience capital consumption, and do pay indirect business taxes. The answers to Problem 2 tell us that if there were no capital consumption and no indirect business taxes, GNP from the earnings viewpoint would equal the sum of _____ , _____ ,

_____ , and _____ , or, in other words, the _____ by all firms in the economy. We see from the answers to Problems 3 and 4 that this sum underestimates GNP if firms have _____ or pay _____

_____ .

To estimate GNP from the earnings viewpoint, we must therefore add to the sum of wages, rent, interest, and profit of all firms in the economy the sum of _____

_____ and _____

_____

for these firms.

6. Now we are in a position to see precisely why GNP from the earnings viewpoint must equal GNP from the product viewpoint. Consider an economy with only two firms, a producer of peas and a producer of pea soup. Assume that all of the peas produced are intermediate product. Also assume that both firms pay indirect business taxes and experience depreciation of their capital equipment. Their income statements are presented below:

Pea producer		Pea soup producer	
Value of peas produced	$100	Value of pea soup produced	$150
Wages	40	Wages	10
Rent	20	Rent	3
Interest	5	Interest	2
Depreciation	5	Peas	100
Indirect business taxes	5	Depreciation	5
Profit	_____	Indirect business taxes	8
		Profit	_____

(a) GNP from the product viewpoint is $ _____ , which consists of $ _____ of peas and $ _____ of pea soup.

(b) To calculate profit in pea production we subtract the sum of _____ , _____ ,

_____ ,

_____ , and _____

_____

from _____

_____ .

The value of peas now enters as a cost in the production of pea soup. Looking at the income statement for the pea soup producer it is clear that profit is calculated, as always, as a residual, so that the value of pea soup produced *must* equal the total costs of pea soup production, where profit is considered to be a cost. But the value of pea soup in this example is GNP from the product viewpoint. Thus, we may summarize by stating that GNP (the value of pea soup produced) equals the sum of:

(1) _____ ;

(2) _____ ;

(3) _____ ;

(4) _____ ;

(5) _____ ;

(6) _____ ;

(7) the value of peas used in the production of pea soup.

But the value of peas used equals the sum of:

(1) _____ ;

(2) _____ ;

(3) _____ ;

(4) _____ ;

(5) _____ ;

(6) _____

in the production of peas.

Combining these, we see that GNP equals the sum of:

(1) _____ ;

(2) _____ ;

(3) _____ ;

(4) _____ ;

(5) _____ ;

(6) _____

at all stages of production.

Thus, GNP from the earnings viewpoint *must* equal GNP from the product viewpoint *because* profit is calculated as a residual. In fact, GNP in our economy from the earnings viewpoint is calculated exactly as above except that it is broken down more finely.

7. Fill in the following table. (*Hint:* Be sure that you understand and note the difference between net investment and gross investment.)

Item	Year 1	Year 2	Year 3
Personal consumption expenditures	$115	$140	$____
Rental income of persons	3	4	5
Corporate profits before taxes	25	31	45
Net investment	25	____	27
Proprietors' income	20	30	
Compensation of employees	100	____	120
Indirect business taxes	13	14	14
Imports	1	5	3
Government purchases of goods and services	____	30	20
Net interest	1	1	3
Capital consumption allowances	15	16	____
Exports	3	2	3
GNP	____	206	225
NNP	____		207
NI	____	____	____

8. Use the following information to answer questions (a), (b), and (c) below.

Wages and salaries	$150
Transfer payments (including interest)	26
Indirect business taxes	25
Undistributed corporate profits	15
Rental income of persons	10
Corporation profits before taxes	35
Capital consumption allowances	18
Corporate income taxes	15
Personal income taxes	45
Proprietors' income	30
Social security contributions	15
Net interest	5
Corporation dividends	5

(a) Calculate:

GNP $ _____

NNP $ _____

NI $ _____

PI $ _____

DPI $ _____

(b) If you had not been given the amount of undistributed corporate profits, could you have computed it given the rest of the information above? _____ If so, how would you do this? If not, why not? _____

_____

_____

_____

(c) If the above data are for Year 1 and if prices in Year 1 are 80 percent of prices in Year 3, express GNP and *DPI* of Year 1 in prices of Year 3.

GNP: $ _____ , *DPI*: $ _____

SELF-TEST: TRUE–FALSE QUESTIONS

Circle T if the statement is true, F if it is false. (Answers are given at the end of the chapter.)

T F 1. GNP measures the total market value of all goods and services produced in the economy during a year.

T F 2. GNP is expressed in money terms because value is the common denominator which permits us to add a collection of heterogeneous items.

T F 3. If GNP in Year 1 is $100 and GNP in Year 2 is $120, we know that society as a whole is better off in Year 2 than it was in Year 1.

T F 4. If both prices and physical output were lower in 1933 than in 1946, then 1946 output expressed in 1933 prices must be less than 1933 output expressed in 1933 prices.

T F 5. If we know current dollar GNP for 1969, we may express this in constant dollars by dividing current dollar GNP by the appropriate price index.

T F 6. By double counting we mean including the same value in the GNP twice instead of once.

T F 7. Although in a very simple economy GNP can be measured in two different ways, this is not even theoretically possible in a complex economy, since what we as individuals receive is not equal to the value of things that we produce.

T F 8. GNP seriously underestimates the value of production in the U.S. economy since it does not take into account the fact that all productive activities do not appear in the marketplace where we collect our data.

T F 9. If we see that real GNP is rising over time, we may say that social welfare must have increased.

T F 10. By the social costs of production we mean the real (if unmeasurable) costs that accrue to society as a whole as a by-product of the production process but which do not necessarily accrue to producers directly as part of their costs of production.

T F 11. Personal consumption expenditures include all expenditures made by households.

T F 12. The value of newly produced consumer goods sold does not necessarily equal the value of newly produced consumer goods produced. If it does not, the value of consumer goods produced but not sold appears in the GNP accounts in the entry "Gross Private Domestic Investment."

T F 13. When a corporation issues stock or bonds, it uses the money it receives to purchase capital equipment. Since capital equipment is productive, the exclusion of business sales of stock and bonds from the GNP accounts results in a GNP which underestimates the value of final products produced.

T F 14. The value added by a firm to the GNP equals the sum of the wages, interest, and rent it pays.

T F 15. When a business firm decides to sell a machine that it has been using to another business firm, the value of the sale is *not* included in the GNP.

T F 16. Gross private domestic investment cannot be smaller than net private domestic investment.

T F 17. Indirect business taxes should not be included when calculating the GNP because they tend to be shifted forward to consumers.

T F 18. Although depreciation is not a cost to business firms in the sense that they have to make a cash outlay each year for depreciation charges, it is nonetheless a cost because it represents the gradual deterioration of their capital stock.

T F 19. GNP from the earnings viewpoint equals the sum of wages, rent, interest, profit, indirect business taxes, and depreciation at the final stage of production.

T F 20. NNP really measures the market value of final goods and services produced during the year, adjusted for the value of capital consumed in the production process during the year.

T F 21. In an economy in which the government did not collect taxes and made no expenditures, *NI* would equal NNP but NNP would not necessarily equal GNP.

T F 22. In the State of Euphoria the government does not impose income taxes. In Euphoria, therefore, *DPI* equals *PI*.

SELF-TEST: MULTIPLE-CHOICE QUESTIONS

Circle the letter that corresponds to the best answer. (Answers are given at the end of the chapter.)

1. Which of the following does *not* describe the GNP of an economy?
   (a) *NI* plus indirect business taxes and capital consumption allowances.
   (b) The total market value of final goods and services produced.
   (c) The total market value of all goods and services sold.
   (d) The sum of value added at all stages of production.
   (e) The sum of personal consumption expenditures, gross investment, government expenditures for goods and services, and net exports.

2. If GNP was $1,000 in Year 1 and $1,200 in Year 2, and prices were higher in Year 2 than they were in Year 1, then:
   (a) Real GNP was larger in Year 1 than it was in Year 2.
   (b) Real GNP was larger in Year 2 than it was in Year 1.
   (c) Real NNP was smaller in Year 2 than it was in Year 1.
   (d) *DPI* must have been larger in Year 2 than it was in Year 1.
   (e) We cannot say in which year either real GNP, NNP, or *DPI* was larger.

3. If GNP was $1,000 in Year 1 and $1,200 in Year 2, and prices were higher in Year 1 than they were in Year 2, then:
   (a) Real GNP was larger in Year 1 than it was in Year 2.
   (b) Real GNP was larger in Year 2 than it was in Year 1.
   (c) Real NNP was smaller in Year 2 than it was in Year 1.
   (d) *DPI* must have been larger in Year 1 than it was in Year 2.
   (e) We cannot say in which year either real GNP or *DPI* was larger.

4. In our economy, GNP equals:
   (a) Value added at all stages of production.
   (b) Value added at all stages of production adjusted for inventory changes.
   (c) An amount which must be less than the value added at all stages of production.
   (d) An amount which must be greater than the value added at all stages of production.
   (e) None of the above.

5. We would be guilty of double counting if we included in the GNP:
   (a) The value of fertilizer used in wheat production.
   (b) The value of wheat included in bread production.
   (c) The value of bread included in prepared stuffing mixes.
   (d) The value of prepared stuffing mixes used in prestuffed turkeys.
   (e) All of the above.

6. An example of a nonproductive market activity is:
   (a) The sale of an intermediate good.
   (b) The services provided by a bank.
   (c) The sale of useless drugs.
   (d) The sale by a household of a used television set.
   (e) The sale of store-damaged merchandise.

7. An example of a productive nonmarket activity is:
   (a) The exchange of gifts during holiday seasons.
   (b) The production of homemade bread.
   (c) Giving "hot tips" on the stock market.
   (d) The services provided by doctors.
   (e) The services provided by stockbrokers.

8. Although the value of such items as cleaning and cooking when done by hired help is included in our GNP, the value of the same items when done by housewives is excluded from our GNP.
   (a) This makes sense because these services are nonproductive anyway.
   (b) It does not make much difference whether housewives' services are included or not since these services would not have much market value.
   (c) This means that, other things remaining the same, when a man marries his housekeeper, the GNP falls!
   (d) This results in the GNP falling over time as more women go to work and hire other people to do their housework for them.
   (e) None of the above.

9. Which of the following is *not* an example of a social cost?
   (a) Air and water pollution.
   (b) Wildlife destroyed when trees are sprayed with DDT.
   (c) The profits earned by farmers using DDT.
   (d) Damage to beaches due to leaking offshore drilling rigs.
   (e) Soil deterioration due to the salting of roads in winter.

10. Which of the following is *not* a reason for real GNP being an imperfect measure of how well off society is?
   (a) It says nothing about *PI* distribution.
   (b) It says nothing about how much social cost is generated in producing the GNP.
   (c) It says nothing about the quality of output.

(d) It says nothing about how much leisure time people have.

(e) It is measured in dollar terms and the purchasing power of money changes over time.

11. Which of the following statements about the relationship between GNP and NNP is true?
(a) NNP is greater than GNP if prices are rising.
(b) NNP is greater than GNP if prices are falling.
(c) NNP *could* be greater than GNP if prices are rising.
(d) NNP *cannot* be greater than GNP.
(e) NNP *must* be greater than GNP.

12. Indirect business taxes:
(a) Include corporate profit taxes.
(b) Include *personal income* taxes.
(c) Include social security taxes.
(d) Include all of the above.
(e) Include none of the above.

CHECKPOINT: LEARNING OBJECTIVES

At this point, you should be able to do all of the following:

1. Explain all of the technical terms and concepts appearing at the end of the chapter in the text.

2. Explain how price changes affect the comparison of GNPs as measures of real output in different years.

3. Deflate current dollar GNP so as to express it in prices of a base period, given the appropriate price index.

4. Calculate the value added by a firm to the GNP, given the necessary data.

5. Explain why GNP is an imperfect measure of society's well-being.

6. Explain why GNP can be measured from both expenditure and income viewpoints, and why both must yield the same result.

7. Explain the difference and relationship between gross private domestic investment and net private domestic investment.

8. Describe what each of the following includes in the product accounts:

(a) Wages.
(b) Rent.
(c) Interest.
(d) Profit.
(e) Indirect business taxes.
(f) Capital consumption allowances.

9. Calculate each of the following, given the necessary data:
(a) GNP
(b) NNP
(c) *NI*
(d) *PI*
(e) *DPI*

QUESTIONS TO THINK ABOUT

1. GNP is an estimate of *final* product produced, but what goods are "final" is to some extent arbitrary. Can you think of some goods which are borderline between being final and intermediate?

2. "It is illogical to call transfer payments such as social security benefits unproductive because in many instances they keep people from starving, and if this is not productive, nothing is!" What is wrong with this statement?

3. Economists frequently define income to mean money *earned* through rendering factor services in the production process. In this sense, *NI* is income but *PI* is not. Why not?

4. Explain what the terms GNP, NNP, *NI*, *PI*, and *DPI* are trying to measure. On the basis of this explanation, show *why* you make the adjustments to GNP that you do in order to arrive at each of the other income measures.

5. Does real GNP tell you more about social welfare than money GNP? When would it and when would it not?

6. Why do you suppose that in discussing economic performance newspapers typically discuss changes in GNP rather than in NNP? Does it make any difference?

7. What would happen to the GNP if each housewife, instead of washing her own kitchen floor, hired her neighbor to do it? Would it make more sense in measuring the GNP to include services of housewives? If so, why isn't it done?

8. Would GNP minus gross national disproduct measure social welfare?

ANSWERS

Answers to Fill-in Questions

1. gross national product
2. transfer payment
3. investment
4. inventories
5. disinvestment
6. capital consumption depreciation
7. national income
8. net national product
9. personal income
10. disposable income
11. value added
12. real
13. current
    constant
14. deflated
15. gross national expenditures

Answers to Problems

1. (a) Value of output in current dollars

       15
       14
       24

   The highest current dollar output occurred in Year 3.

   (b)

Year t	Price in Year t as a % of price in Year 1	Price in Year t as a % of price in Year 2	Price in Year t as a % of price in Year 3
1	100	150	75
2	67	100	50
3	133	200	100

   (c)

Year	Value of output in constant dollars of Year 1	Value of output in constant dollars of Year 2	Value of output in constant dollars of Year 3
1	15	10	20
2	21	14	28
3	18	12	24

   (d) Year 2   Year 2   Year 2
       Year 3   Year 3   Year 3
       Year 1   Year 1   Year 1

   (e) If you are calculating constant-dollar GNP for a group of years, the dollar magnitude depends on which year you select as a base year — the prices of the year in which all GNPs will be expressed. But the *ranking* of the GNPs from largest to smallest does *not* depend on which year you select as a base year.

(f)

Value of GNP in Year 1 in dollars of Year 1 as a % of:	Value of GNP in Year 1 in dollars of Year 2 as a % of:	Value of GNP in Year 1 in dollars of Year 3 as a % of:
Value of GNP in Year 2 in dollars of Year 1 71.4	Value of GNP in Year 2 in dollars of Year 2 71.4	Value of GNP in Year 2 in dollars of Year 3 71.4
Value of GNP in Year 3 in dollars of Year 1 83.3	Value of GNP in Year 3 in dollars of Year 2 83.3	Value of GNP in Year 3 in dollars of Year 3 83.3

   (g) Regardless of the year you select as a base, the relationship between constant-dollar GNPs of different years will be the same.

2. (a) Profit in fertilizer firm $ 1
       Profit in apple firm $ 5
       Profit in cider firm $10
   (b) $0
       $60
       $30
       $90
   (c) wages
       rent
       interest
       profit
       $90

3. (a) Profit: $25
   (b) $100
   (c) depreciation
       cost
       wages
       rent
       interest
       profit
       depreciation
       all
       all

4. (a) Profit: $55
   (b) $200
   (c) indirect business taxes
          (a property tax)
       cost
       wages
       rent
       interest
       profit
       indirect business taxes

all

all

5. wages

rent

interest

profit

value added

depreciation

indirect business taxes

depreciation

indirect business taxes

6. Pea producer's profit $25

  Pea soup producer's profit $22

  (a) $150

       $0

       $150

  (b)   wages

       rent

       interest

       depreciation

       indirect business taxes

       the value of peas produced

  (1)   Wages

  (2)   Rent

  (3)   Interest

  (4)   Profit

  (5)   Depreciation

  (6)   Indirect business taxes

  (1)   Wages

  (2)   Rent

  (3)   Interest

  (4)   Profit

  (5)   Depreciation

  (6)   Indirect business taxes

  (1)   Wages

  (2)   Rent

  (3)   Interest

  (4)   Profit

  (5)   Depreciation

  (6)   Indirect business taxes

7. *Year 1*

  Government purchases of goods and services $ 20

  GNP   177

NNP   162

NI   149

Year 2

Net investment $ 23

Compensation of employees   110

NNP   190

NI   176

Year 3

Personal consumption expenditures $160

Proprietors' income   20

Capital consumption allowances   18

NI   193

8. (a)   GNP $273

       NNP   255

       NI   230

       PI   211

       DPI   166

  (b)   Yes. Subtract dividends and corporate income taxes from total corporate profits.

  (c)   GNP $341.25

       DPI   207.50

Answers to True–False Questions

1.	F	9.	F	16.	T
2.	T	10.	T	17.	F
3.	F	11.	F	18.	T
4.	F	12.	T	19.	F
5.	T	13.	F	20.	T
6.	T	14.	F	21.	T
7.	F	15.	T	22.	T
8.	F				

Answers to Multiple-Choice Questions

1.	c	5.	e	9.	c
2.	e	6.	d	10.	e
3.	b	7.	b	11.	d
4.	a	8.	c	12.	e

CHAPTER 8

Economic Instability: Unemployment and Inflation

CHAPTER ORIENTATION

This chapter develops and explains the following concepts:

The definition of business cycles and the characteristics of the four phases of each cycle.

Different methods of economic forecasting.

What is meant by "the labor force" and "unemployment," and the different types of unemployment that exist in our economy.

The definition of inflation, different types of inflation that occur, and the effects of inflation on different groups of people.

FILL-IN QUESTIONS

Complete the following sentences. (Answers are given at the end of the chapter.)

1. The recurrent but nonperiodic fluctuations in general economic activity that take place over a period of years are called _____.

2. The fluctuations in sales and economic activity during particular periods of the year, such as Christmas, are called _____ fluctuations.

3. The upper phase of a business cycle in which the economy is operating at or near full employment is called _____ _____. When income, output, and employment decrease, the downward phase is called _____ and will continue until the lowest phase is reached, which is called _____ _____. When the economy picks up again, the upward phase is called _____ _____.

4. Time series that tend to move ahead of aggregate economic activity are called _____ indicators, whereas those that tend to follow or trail behind aggregate

economic activity are called _____ indicators.

5. All people 16 years of age or older who are either employed or unemployed but seeking work constitute the economy's _____.

6. Unemployment of a short-run nature resulting from imperfect labor mobility, imperfect knowledge of job opportunities, and the economy's inability to match people with jobs instantly is called _____ _____ unemployment. Unemployment that results from business recessions and depressions is called _____ unemployment. And unemployment that results from fundamental economic and social changes within the economy which prevent people from getting jobs because of inadequate education, race, age, obsolete skills, and so forth is called _____ unemployment.

7. When people who want to work are unable to find jobs at going wage rates for their given skills and experiences, we say that _____ unemployment exists.

8. A rise in the general level of prices of all goods and services is called _____. When prices rise because aggregate demand is rising faster than the economy's ability to supply goods, we say that _____ inflation exists. When prices rise because factor payments to one or more groups of resource owners rise faster than productivity, we say that _____ _____ inflation exists.

9. The _____ is a weighted average of prices of goods and services commonly purchased by working-class families in urban areas. The _____

_____ is a weighted average of selected items priced in wholesale markets, including raw materials, semifinished products, and finished goods.

10. The purchasing power of money income as measured by the quantity of goods and services that can be bought with it is called _____.

PROBLEMS

(Answers are given at the end of the chapter.)

1. What type of unemployment do you think each of the following situations represents? Use F to designate "frictional," C to designate "cyclical," and S to designate "structural."

   (a) A person quits a job and has to wait a few weeks before finding another. _____

   (b) Skilled workers are replaced by machines and find that their skills are nontransferable. _____

   (c) An assembly-line worker is laid off because of a factory slowdown caused by generally lagging sales. _____

   (d) A former college professor sells apples on a corner during the Great Depression. _____

   (e) A miner in Appalachia becomes unemployed when a different energy source permanently replaces the use of coal. _____

2. Because inflation may be caused by many different factors, a policy that successfully curbed one inflation may not be helpful to fight another. Below is a list of policies. For which type or types of inflation would each be most appropriate (regardless of their desirability for other reasons)?

   (a) Reducing aggregate demand by increasing personal income taxes. _____

   _____

   (b) Restricting wage increases so that they do not exceed productivity gains. _____

   _____

   (c) Forcing corporations to adjust prices so as to maintain a fixed margin of profit. _____

_____

(d) Increasing the competitiveness of both big businesses

and big unions. _____

_____

_____ .

3. At a given point in time your balance sheet is as follows:

Assets		Liabilities and Net Worth	
Cash	$ 500	Mortgage	$19,000
House	20,000	Net worth	1,500
	$20,500		$20,500

(a) If prices rise by 5 percent, the value of your house
increases correspondingly, you make no mortgage
payments, and you do not spend your cash, your
balance sheet would be:

Assets		Liabilities and Net Worth	
Cash	$ _____	Mortgage	$ _____
House	_____	Net worth	_____

(b) You net worth in preinflation dollars would be

$ _____ . You have therefore (gained/lost/

neither gained nor lost) _____ from

inflation. And this makes sense because in fact you are

a net (debtor/creditor) _____ .

4. At a point in time your balance sheet is as follows:

Assets		Liabilities and Net Worth	
Cash	$200	Debt	$300
Notes receivable	400	Net worth	300
	$600		$600

(a) If prices rise by 5 percent and you have neither paid
off your debt nor received payments on your notes,
your balance sheet would be:

Assets		Liabilities and Net Worth	
Cash	$ _____	Debt	$ _____
Notes receivable	_____	Net worth	_____

(b) Your net worth in preinflation dollars would be

$ _____ . You have therefore (gained/lost/neither

gained nor lost) _____ from inflation. And

this makes sense because you are in fact a net (debtor/

creditor) _____ .

SELF-TEST: TRUE–FALSE QUESTIONS

*Circle T if the statement is true, F if it is false. (Answers
are given at the end of the chapter.)*

T F 1. Business cycles are recurrent but nonperiodic
fluctuations in the level of economic activity.

T F 2. The four phases of business cycles are usually
equal in scope and intensity.

T F 3. The upswings in economic activity that pre-
cede Christmas and Easter would *not* be called
business cycles.

T F 4. There does not appear to be any systematic
relationship between the level of economic
activity and movements in prices.

T F 5. The reason that the production of durable
goods fluctuates more than the production of
nondurable goods is that durable goods tend
to be less essential than nondurable goods.

T F 6. Hard-goods industries in general are more
competitive than soft-goods industries.

T F 7. A change that occurs in the birth rate will not
show up in the labor force statistics for 16
years.

T F 8. Some frictional unemployment is inevitable in
an economy like ours where people are free to
seek the type of employment they wish.

T F 9. Elimination of the business cycle would not
eliminate cyclical unemployment because
seasonal needs for labor would still exist.

T F 10. Structural unemployment could not exist if the
labor force were homogeneous and fully mobile.

T F 11. Hard-core unemployment would be eliminated
if we could reduce total unemployment to less
than 5 percent.

T F 12. Mr. S. insists on a wage of $10 per hour. The
best job available in his line of work pays only
$5 per hour. If he does not accept this job, he
is, by definition, involuntarily unemployed.

T F 13. If during an inflationary period wages rise, we know that inflation is due to cost push.

T F 14. Market-power inflation is more likely to occur when the economy does not have substantial unemployment.

T F 15. If during an inflation both profits and wages are rising, the inflation must be due to excess aggregate demand.

SELF-TEST: MULTIPLE-CHOICE QUESTIONS

Circle the letter that corresponds to the best answer. (Answers are given at the end of the chapter.)

1. Which of the following is *not* a phase of the business cycle?
   (a) Inflation.
   (b) Depression.
   (c) Recovery.
   (d) Prosperity.
   (e) Recession.

2. Which of the following industries would you expect to experience the most substantial changes in employment and output over the business cycle?
   (a) Food.
   (b) Clothing.
   (c) Automobiles.
   (d) Medical services.
   (e) Education.

3. The demand for durable goods fluctuates more than the demand for nondurable goods because:
   (a) Durable goods tend to be luxuries and the demand for luxuries is more income-sensitive than is the demand for necessities.
   (b) Durable goods are durable by definition, and their purchase can be postponed when income falls.
   (c) Durable goods are less competitive for the consumers' dollar than are nondurable goods.
   (d) Durable goods become difficult to get as output declines because producers cut back their production before they cut back the production of nondurable goods.
   (e) Durable goods are expensive, and so the use of their services is the "first thing to go" when income falls.

4. The production of durable goods fluctuates more than the production of nondurable goods because:
   (a) The demand for durable goods is less income-sensitive than the demand for nondurable goods.

   (b) The demand for durable goods is less price-sensitive than the demand for nondurable goods.
   (c) The durable goods industry is very competitive and producers therefore overrespond to changes in demand.
   (d) The durable goods industry is not very competitive, so changes in demand can be met by changes in output without substantial changes in prices.
   (e) Durable goods producers are very "bearish" and cut prices at the first sign of weakening markets.

5. Which of the following people would *not* technically be included in the labor force?
   (a) A 42-year-old man who does not currently have a job but who is looking for one.
   (b) A PFC in the Army.
   (c) A 13-year-old who has a paper route.
   (d) A woman working to put her husband through college.
   (e) A movie star who is "between pictures."

6. When full employment exists:
   (a) Everybody is working.
   (b) There is a very high level of employment, with the unemployed being largely frictionally unemployed.
   (c) Frictional unemployment is virtually zero.
   (d) About 4 percent of the labor force is structurally unemployed.
   (e) The only people who are unemployed are those who refuse to accept jobs at the going wage.

7. The measured overall unemployment rate:
   (a) Includes as unemployed all housewives and students, regardless of whether or not they are seeking employment.
   (b) Does *not* include as unemployed people who have become discouraged and have given up trying to find work, even though they want to be employed.
   (c) Reflects the fact that some people are only partially employed.
   (d) Includes only people over 18 years of age.
   (e) Cannot indicate the direction in which unemployment is changing over time.

8. "Normal" unemployment will tend to rise:
   (a) If the proportion of teenagers in the labor force declines.
   (b) If the proportion of women in the labor force declines.
   (c) If the minimum-wage rate increases.
   (d) Whenever the rate of technological advance declines.
   (e) Whenever the population increases.

9. The economic cost of unemployment:
   (a) Is the output forgone that could have been produced had the labor force been fully employed.

(b) Tends to be reduced through welfare payments.

(c) Is the degradation and unrest that results when a substantial part of the labor force is unemployed.

(d) Runs about $7 billion annually.

(e) Is not large because losses in depression periods are offset by gains in prosperity periods.

10. Inflation exists whenever:

(a) All prices are rising.

(b) The purchasing power of money is falling.

(c) The average level of prices is rising although some prices may be falling.

(d) It becomes increasingly expensive to maintain a given standard of living.

(e) All of the above.

11. Which of the following is *not* true with regard to inflation?

(a) Cost-push inflation implies that rising prices are due to wages increasing faster than productivity and/or to business firms trying to increase their profit margins.

(b) Market-power inflation can occur without excess aggregate demand.

(c) Demand-pull inflation places the blame for rising prices on the fact that demand is in excess of the output that the economy can produce at or near full employment.

(d) Demand-pull inflation occurs whenever aggregate demand increases.

(e) Cost-push inflation may be a continuing problem if the economy is to maintain a high level of income and employment.

12. If prices and wages are both increasing and the unemployment rate is 8 percent:

(a) We are experiencing demand inflation.

(b) We are experiencing wage-push inflation.

(c) We are experiencing profit-push inflation.

(d) We are probably experiencing some kind of cost-push inflation, but we do not know which kind.

(e) There is not enough information to tell.

13. A person will tend to be hurt by inflation in the sense that his real net worth will decline if:

(a) His real assets equal his real liabilities and he has no monetary assets or liabilities.

(b) He has only monetary assets and real liabilities.

(c) He has only real assets and monetary liabilities.

(d) He has only monetary liabilities and no assets.

(e) He has no assets or liabilities.

14. Unanticipated inflation:

(a) Tends to redistribute wealth arbitrarily.

(b) Harms stockholders of nonfinancial business firms which are net monetary debtors.

(c) Benefits households which are net monetary creditors.

(d) Helps fixed-income recipients who are neither debtors nor creditors.

(e) Redistributes wealth from debtors to creditors.

CHECKPOINT: LEARNING OBJECTIVES

At this point you should be able to do all of the following:

1. Explain all of the technical terms and concepts listed at the end of the chapter in the text.

2. Describe the relationship between actual GNP and its trend over time.

3. Describe the behavior of output, employment, and prices in durable and nondurable goods industries over the business cycle, and explain why this behavior exists.

4. Describe each of the following methods of forecasting:

(a) Mechanical extrapolation.

(b) Opinion polling.

(c) Econometric models.

(d) Economic indicators.

5. Discuss the factors causing:

(a) Frictional unemployment.

(b) Cyclical unemployment.

(c) Structural unemployment.

6. Explain why the "normal" unemployment level is likely to increase over time, and describe the economic and social costs of unemployment.

7. Explain the difference between demand-pull and cost-push or market-power inflation.

8. Distinguish between different types of market-power inflation.

9. Explain and illustrate how unanticipated inflation redistributes wealth from people who are net monetary creditors to people who are net monetary debtors.

10. Calculate the change in a person's real net worth due to price-level changes, given his balance sheet and price-level data.

QUESTIONS TO THINK ABOUT

1. If a series leads one business cycle, it must lag the preceding cycle. What sense does it make, then, to distinguish between leading and lagging indicators?

2. What types of factors would tend to make mechanical extrapolation an inaccurate method of forecasting? What factors would make opinion polling inaccurate?

3. Assume that you were trying to explain why an economy was experiencing inflation and could get any data you wanted. What data would you want? How would you use it? Do you think you could determine what was causing the inflation? How?

4. If you as a policy maker had to choose between, say, 5 percent unemployment and 3 percent inflation per year or 3½ percent unemployment and 6 percent inflation per year, which would you select? Why?

5. Is the redistribution of income and wealth which occurs during inflation really unjust? Why or why not?

ANSWERS

Answers to Fill-in Questions

1. business cycles
2. seasonal
3. prosperity
   recession
   depression
   recovery
4. leading
   lagging
5. labor force

6. frictional
   cyclical
   structural
7. involuntary
8. inflation
   demand-pull
   cost-push *or* market-power
9. consumer price index
   wholesale price index
10. real income

Answers to Problems

1. (a) F
   (b) S
   (c) C
   (d) C
   (e) S

2. (a) Demand-pull inflation
   (b) Wage-push inflation
   (c) Profit-push inflation
   (d) Market-power inflation — wage-push and profit-push

3. (a)

Assets		Liabilities and Net Worth	
Cash	$ 500	Mortgage	$19,000
House	21,000	Net worth	2,500

   (b) $2,380.95
        gained
        debtor

4. (a)

Assets		Liabilities and Net Worth	
Cash	$ 200	Debt	$ 300
Notes receivable	400	Net worth	300

   (b) $285.71
        lost
        creditor

Answers to True–False Questions

1.	T	6.	F	11.	F
2.	F	7.	T	12.	F
3.	T	8.	T	13.	F
4.	F	9.	F	14.	T
5.	F	10.	T	15.	F

Answers to Multiple-Choice Questions

1.	a	9.	a
2.	c	10.	e
3.	b	11.	d (For demand-pull inflation to occur, the economy must be at or near full employment.)
4.	d		
5.	c		
6.	b	12.	d
7.	b	13.	b
8.	c	14.	a

CHAPTER 9

Consumption, Saving, and Investment: Elements of the Theory of Income and Employment

CHAPTER ORIENTATION

This chapter develops and explains the following concepts:

The classical theory of income and employment, which viewed supply as always creating its own demand so that if markets were competitive, full employment would tend to prevail.

Keynes's criticisms of the classical theory, which led to the conclusion that the economy's maintaining full employment would be the exception rather than the rule.

The theory of consumption, which states that consumption demand depends primarily on the level of disposable income.

The theory of investment, which states that the investment demand curve depends on the expected yield on additions to the capital stock, and that the amount of investment that firms plan to undertake during a period is determined by the expected yield and the market rate of interest.

FILL-IN QUESTIONS

Complete the following sentences. (Answers are given at the end of the chapter.)

1. The idea that supply creates its own demand is known as _____ .

2. The total value of output that all sectors of the economy are willing to purchase is called _____ .

3. The amount of income which is not consumed is said to be _____ .

4. The body of theory developed by pre-Keynesian economists which showed that the economy would automatically tend toward full employment through the free operation of the price system is called _____ economics.

5. Expenditures on consumer goods and services are called _____ .

6. The relation between consumption and income is called the _____ or the _____ .

7. The relation between saving and income is called the

_____

or the _____

_____ .

8. The ratio of consumption to income is called the _____

_____

_____ . The ratio of saving to income

is called the _____

_____ .

9. The change in consumption resulting from a unit change in

income is called the _____

_____ .

The change in saving resulting from a unit change in income

is called the _____

_____ .

10. A movement along the consumption function is called a

change in _____

_____ . A movement along the

saving function is called a change in _____

_____ .

11. An upward or downward shift in the consumption function

is called a change in _____ .

An upward or downward shift in the saving function is

called a change in _____ .

12. Desired additions to plant, equipment, and inventories

constitute _____

demand.

13. The expected rate of return over cost on an additional unit

of a capital good is called the _____

_____ .

PROBLEMS

(Answers are given at the end of the chapter.)

1. **(a)** You are given the following information about dis-

posable income and consumption for a family during a
period of time. Fill in the rest of the columns.

Disposable income	Consumption	Saving	APC	APS	MPC	MPS
$100	$120	$ ____	____	____		
120	130	____	____	____	____	____
140	140	____	____	____	____	____
160	150	____	____	____	____	____
180	160	____	____	____	____	____

Note that the sum of the *APC* and the *APS* equals

_____ and that the sum of the *MPC* and the *MPS*

equals _____ .

(b) In the first graph below, plot the consumption–income
relationship and in the second graph draw the saving–
income relationship. (Be sure to label both axes and
graphs.)

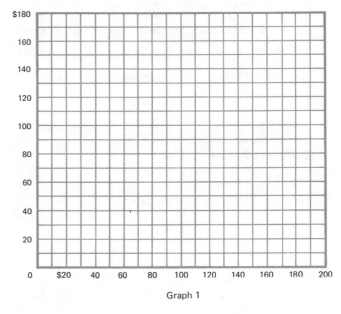

Graph 1

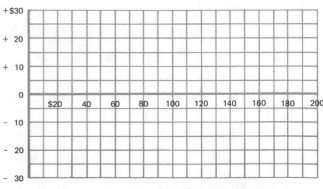

Graph 2

(c) Now indicate the break-even point on each graph by the letter A.

(d) In the first graph, the MPC is measured as the

_____ of the _____

_____.

In the second graph, the MPS is measured as the

_____ of the _____

_____.

2. What effect would you expect each of the following to have on the consumption function? Use a $(+)$ to indicate an upward shift in the function, a (0) to indicate no change, and a $(-)$ to indicate a downward shift.

(a) A decrease in the volume of liquid assets that people

own. _____

(b) An increase in disposable income. _____

(c) People's expectations about future prices changing so

that they now expect prices to rise in the future. _____

(d) The removal of product rationing after a war. _____

(e) An increase in social security benefits. _____

3. Assume that columns (1) and (2) of the following table refer to the consumption function of an economy at a given point in time.

(1) DI	(2) C	$C'\left(MPC = \dfrac{1}{2}\right)$	C''
$100	$ 80	$ _____	$ _____
120	95	_____	_____
140	110	_____	_____
160	125	_____	_____
180	140	_____	_____

(a) The MPC is _____.

(b) Assume that the following change in the consumption function occurs: the MPC becomes $\dfrac{1}{2}$, but at $DI =$ $100, consumption remains $80. Using this information, fill in column C' to describe the new relationship between DI and consumption.

(c) This change results in (an increase/no change/a decrease) _____ in the APC at the $100 level of DI.

(d) In the space below, draw the original consumption function and the one derived in part (b). Label them C and C'. Explain in words what this graph tells you.

DISPOSABLE INCOME

_____

_____

_____

_____

_____

_____

_____

(e) Now assume that there is a change in consumption such that the MPC is what it was originally but that at $DI =$ $100 the APC is 0.9. Using this information, fill in column C'' in the table shown at the beginning of this problem.

(f) Add the consumption function you derived in part (e) to the graph above and label it C''.

(g) Looking at the relationship between C and C', explain how a change in the MPC affects the consumption function. And looking at the relationship between C and C'', explain how a change in the APC with no change in the MPC affects the consumption function.

_____

_____

_____

_____

4. Firms A, B, and C are each considering undertaking several different investment projects. The cost of each project and

its *MEI* are given below. Assume that these are the only three firms in the economy.

Firm A			Firm B			Firm C		
Project	Cost	*MEI* (%)	Project	Cost	*MEI* (%)	Project	Cost	*MEI* (%)
1	$ 800	12	1	$1,000	10	1	$600	14
2	1,200	8	2	800	12	2	800	8
			3	1,200	7			

(a) In the space provided, draw the *MEI* curve for each firm and for the three firms together.

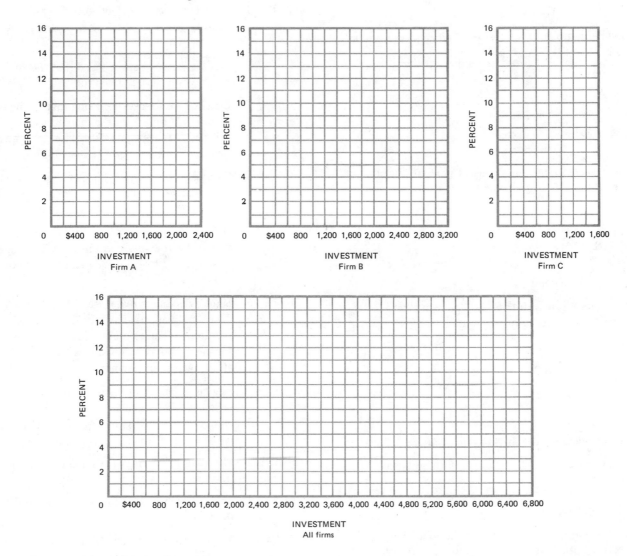

(b) If "percent" as measured vertically refers to the

interest rate, then the *MEI* curve for each firm is its

_____ for investment,
and the *MEI* for all three firms combined is the

_____

_____ .

(c) If the market rate of interest is 15 percent, the amount
of investment that firms plan to undertake is:

Firm A $ _____

Firm B   _____

Firm C   _____

Total   _____

(d) If the market rate of interest is 13 percent, the amount
of investment that firms plan to undertake is:

Firm A $ _____

Firm B   _____

Firm C   _____

Total   _____

(e) If the market rate of interest is 11 percent, the amount
of investment that firms plan to undertake is:

Firm A $ _____

Firm B   _____

Firm C   _____

Total   _____

(f) If the market rate of interest is 6 percent, the amount
of investment that firms plan to undertake is:

Firm A $ _____

Firm B   _____

Firm C   _____

Total   _____

(g) Thus, the higher is the market rate of interest, the

(greater/less) _____ is the amount of

investment that firms will want to undertake, given

the total *MEI* curve.

5. What effect would you expect each of the following to have
on the aggregate *MEI* curve? Use a (+) to indicate a shift to
the right, a (0) to indicate no effect, and a (−) to indicate a
shift to the left.

(a) A reduction in corporate income tax rates. _____

(b) Rapid technological change. _____

(c) An increase in the cost of new capital goods. _____

(d) An increase in expected product demand. _____

(e) An increase in the market rate of interest. _____

*Circle T if the statement is true, F if it is false. (Answers
are given at the end of the chapter.)*

T F   1. Say's Law says, in effect, that demand creates
its own supply, so insufficient demand cannot
exist.

T F   2. Classical economists believed that the economy
would never deviate from full employment.

T F   3. Classical economists, knowing that saving is a
leakage of funds from the income stream,
believed that aggregate demand would equal
aggregate output only if people did not save.

T F   4. Classical economists did not believe that unemployment was a problem because they
believed the labor market to be competitive.

T F   5. One of Keynes's major contributions was
showing that at any point in time, aggregate
income earned need not equal aggregate output
produced.

T F   6. Since a decline in real wages within a single
firm is unlikely to affect the demand for its
product, it follows that a decline in real wages
for the economy as a whole is unlikely to
affect aggregate demand.

T F   7. Aggregate demand is unaffected if planned
saving and investment change by the same
amount and in the same direction, other things
remaining the same.

T F   8. The most important determinant of consumption spending is disposable income.

T F   9. The ratio of consumption to income is called
the *MPC*.

T F 10. The relationship *MPC* + *MPS* = 1 may not be
true if inflationary expectations cause a marked
upward shift in the consumption function.

T F 11. Since *MPC* + *MPS* = 1 and *APC* + *APS* = 1, it
follows that *MPC* = *APC* and *MPS* = *APS*.

T F 12. Engel's laws basically contradict the consumption function hypothesis.

T F 13. Modern economists believe that the major determinant of saving is the rate of return a family can get on its funds.

T F 14. An increase in the *APS* is really the same thing as a decrease in the *APC*.

T F 15. A shift in the consumption function could be caused by many factors, whereas a change in the amount consumed could be caused only by a change in income.

T F 16. If the expected rate of return on investment increases, the amount of investment that firms want to undertake will increase, remain the same, or decrease, depending on what happens to the market rate of interest.

T F 17. An increase in the *MEI* is usually accompanied by an increase in the *MPS* because people want to take advantage of the improved yield on capital.

T F 18. Net foreign demand is the only component of our aggregate demand which can be directly and substantially influenced by policies of other countries.

SELF-TEST: MULTIPLE-CHOICE QUESTIONS

Circle the letter that corresponds to the best answer. (Answers are given at the end of the chapter.)

1. Say's Law of markets states that:
   (a) Markets are competitive.
   (b) Markets are always in equilibrium.
   (c) There cannot be continued general overproduction because supply creates its own demand.
   (d) Capitalistic markets are barter markets.
   (e) Saving equals investment.

2. In the classical macroeconomic model:
   (a) Aggregate supply is equal to aggregate demand because people do not save.
   (b) Aggregate supply is not equal to aggregate demand if business firms invest.
   (c) Aggregate supply will tend to equal aggregate demand because saving will tend to equal investment.
   (d) Aggregate supply will not usually equal aggregate demand because there is no mechanism to equilibrate saving and investment.

(e) Aggregate supply will always equal aggregate demand regardless of whether saving equals investment.

3. In the classical macroeconomic model:
   (a) Full employment will tend to prevail because the labor market is competitive.
   (b) The labor market will tend to be in equilibrium, but there is no assurance that the equilibrium level of employment will be the "full-employment" level.
   (c) Saving will not tend to equal investment because each is undertaken by a different group for a different reason.
   (d) It may be necessary for the government to guide the economy toward full employment.
   (e) Overproduction of specific commodities cannot occur.

4. The Great Depression of the 1930s:
   (a) Could be cured, argued classical economists, if labor and business permitted wages and prices to be flexible and if the government would stop interfering with the market process.
   (b) Confirmed the classical economists' hypothesis of the economy tending toward but not necessarily always being at full employment.
   (c) Was predicted by the Keynesian economists of the day.
   (d) Probably would have occurred even if aggregate demand were equal to full-employment aggregate output.
   (e) Probably would not have occurred had the government followed a policy of laissez-faire.

5. Economists use the term "aggregate demand" to mean:
   (a) The sum of the demand for all products and factor services.
   (b) Household demand for all consumption goods.
   (c) Business demand for all investment goods.
   (d) Demand for all final goods and services.
   (e) Demand for all products except exports.

6. Saving and investment:
   (a) Both fluctuate a great deal from year to year.
   (b) Are both components of aggregate demand.
   (c) Occur primarily in the business sector.
   (d) Occur primarily in the household sector.
   (e) Are done by different groups of people for different reasons.

7. Business saving:
   (a) Derives primarily from new stock issue.
   (b) Is undertaken primarily for the purpose of investment.
   (c) Equals business profits.
   (d) Is greater than household saving during periods of depression when disposable income is low.
   (e) Is so small that for all intents and purposes it is nonexistent.

8. Modern theory concludes that:
   (a) Supply creates its own demand.
   (b) The economy would tend toward full employment if the government would only pursue a policy of laissez-faire.
   (c) Aggregate demand determines the level of output and employment.
   (d) The level of output and employment depend on the level of prices.
   (e) Planned saving always equals planned investment.

9. Engel's Laws:
   (a) State that the most important factor influencing a family's consumption is its level of disposable income.
   (b) State that supply creates its own demand and vice versa.
   (c) Refer to changes in the percentage of income spent on different types of goods as income increases.
   (d) State that demand varies inversely with price.
   (e) Refer to changes in the demands for food, shelter, and clothing which occur over time due to changes in relative prices.

10. Which of the following is *not* true about the relationship between aggregate consumption and income?
    (a) As income increases, the amount consumed increases but by less than the increase in income.
    (b) As income increases, the amounts consumed and saved both increase.
    (c) As income increases, the amount consumed increases more than does the amount saved if the *MPC* is greater than $\frac{1}{2}$.
    (d) As income decreases, the decrease in the sum of the amount consumed and the amount saved exactly equals the decrease in income.
    (e) As income increases, the amount consumed increases by the same amount as the increase in income.

11. Which of the following is *not* necessarily true?
    (a) $MPC + MPS = 1$.
    (b) $APC + APS = 1$.
    (c) $APC + APS = MPC + MPS$.
    (d) $APC = MPC$.
    (e) $C/Y + S/Y = 1$.

12. The difference between the concepts "a change in the amount consumed" and a "change in consumption" is that:
    (a) The former refers to a change in consumption spending induced by a change in income, whereas the latter refers to a change in consumption spending induced by anything but a change in income.
    (b) The former refers to empirical consumption functions,
    whereas the latter refers to theoretical consumption functions.
    (c) The former refers to changes in consumption over a period of time, whereas the latter refers to a change in consumption at a point in time.
    (d) The former refers to a change in consumption spending induced by anything but a change in income, whereas the latter refers to a change in consumption spending due to a change in income.
    (e) There is no difference between the two concepts.

13. Which of the following will not cause a shift in the *MEI*?
    (a) A change in expected demand for a product.
    (b) A change in the interest rate firms must pay on borrowed funds.
    (c) A new union contract which substantially alters real wages.
    (d) A change in the corporate profits tax rate.
    (e) A sharp decrease in consumer spending.

14. The *MEI* is:
    (a) The cost of capital to a firm.
    (b) The expected rate of return on investment.
    (c) The profit a firm earns on its capital stock.
    (d) The additional investment that will occur with an increase in profit.
    (e) The additional investment that will occur with an increase in business optimism.

15. The higher the market rate of interest, other things being equal:
    (a) The lower the rate of investment.
    (b) The lower the *MEI*.
    (c) The higher the rate of investment.
    (d) The higher the *MEI*.
    (e) The steeper the *MEI*.

16. Investment tends to fluctuate from year to year because:
    (a) The things that influence it tend to fluctuate.
    (b) If you buy much capital one year you do not need much the next year.
    (c) Business firms are not consistent in their future goals.
    (d) Consumption, the major component of demand, fluctuates a lot.
    (e) Government policies toward business change frequently.

17. Government demand depends to a large extent on:
    (a) The structure of taxes.
    (b) Credit conditions.
    (c) Disposable income.
    (d) The stock of capital.
    (e) Public needs.

At this point you should be able to do all of the following:

1. Define all of the technical terms and concepts listed at the end of the chapter in the text.

2. Explain why the classical economists believed that:
   (a) Aggregate demand equals aggregate income or output.
   (b) Saving equals investment.
   (c) All markets adjust to their individual full-employment equilibrium levels.

3. State what Keynes believed determines the level of real output.

4. Explain why planned saving need not equal planned investment.

5. Explain why a reduction in wages relative to prices need not restore full employment in an underemployed economy.

6. List some determinants of consumption demand, and state which is the most important.

7. Derive the following, given the relationship between *DI* and *C*:
   (a) *S*
   (b) *APC*
   (c) *APS*
   (d) *MPC*
   (e) *MPS*

8. Construct a propensity-to-save curve from a propensity-to-consume curve, and vice versa.

9. Describe and explain the relationship between the *APC* and the *APS* and between the *MPC* and the *MPS*.

10. Explain what causes a change in consumption and a change in the amount consumed.

11. Describe the consumption–income relationship revealed by:
    (a) (Short-run) budget studies.
    (b) (Long-run) time-series data.

12. Explain why a firm's *MEI* curve is its demand curve for investment.

13. Describe and explain the relationship between investment demand and the market rate of interest.

14. Derive an aggregate *MEI* from individual firms' *MEI*s.

15. Explain how each of the following influences the *MEI* curve:
    (a) Expected product demand.
    (b) Technology and innovation.
    (c) The cost of new capital goods.
    (d) Corporate income tax rates.

16. Describe why the *MEI* tends to be continuously shifting.

17. State the major determinant of government demand.

18. List some determinants of net foreign demand.

QUESTIONS TO THINK ABOUT

1. Why were the classical economists so confident that wage flexibility would tend to make the labor force fully employed?

2. Will aggregate demand change if people want to save more and business firms want to invest more and if the planned addition to saving just equals the planned addition to investment?

3. Why did classical economists believe that changes in planned saving would be accompanied by changes in planned investment, whereas modern economists believe that this is not necessarily the case?

4. Occasionally, Congress passes an investment tax credit which allows business firms to subtract from their tax bills an amount based upon their investment during the year. How do you think this affects the *MEI*? Why do you think this is done?

5. Why do you suppose that the consumption function tends to be relatively stable, whereas the *MEI* is not?

6. When you say that a person has become more thrify, are you implying that his *MPS*, his *APS*, or both his *MPS* and his *APS* have increased?

ANSWERS

Answers to Fill-in Questions

1. Say's Law

2. aggregate demand

3. saved

4. classical

5. consumption

6. propensity to consume
   consumption function

7. propensity to save
   saving function

8. average propensity to consume
   average propensity to save

9. marginal propensity to consume
   marginal propensity to save

10. the amount consumed
    the amount saved

11. consumption
    saving

12. investment

13. marginal efficiency of investment

(b), (c)

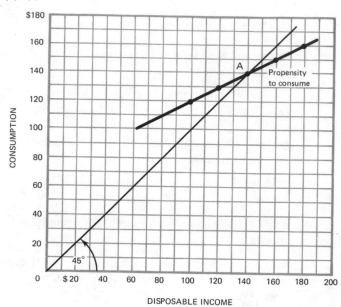

DISPOSABLE INCOME
Graph 1

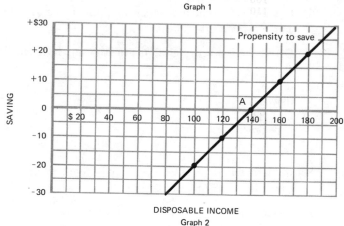

DISPOSABLE INCOME
Graph 2

Answers to Problems

1. (a)

Saving	APC	APS	MPC	MPS
−$20	1.20	−0.2		
			0.5	0.5
− 10	1.08	−0.08		
			0.5	0.5
0	1	0		
			0.5	0.5
10	0.94	0.06		
			0.5	0.5
20	0.89	0.11		

The sum of the *APC* and the *APS* equals 1 and the sum of the *MPC* and the *MPS* equals 1.

(d) slope
consumption function
slope
saving function

2. (a) − (this makes them feel "poorer" − so at any level of *DI* they will try to spend less)
(b) 0 (since only *DI* has changed, there would be a movement along the consumption function)
(c) +
(d) +
(e) 0 (this increases income and the amount consumed, not the consumption function)

3. (a) $\frac{3}{4} = 0.75$

(b)

C'
$ 80
90
100
110
120

(c) no change

(d), (f)

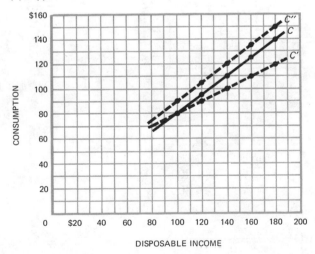

The consumption function has shifted in the following ways:
1. The *MPC* (slope) of C' is less than the *MPC* (slope) of *C*.
2. When *DI* is less than $100, *C* is lower than C'. Thus, for *DI* less than $100, the *APC* corresponding to *C* is less than the *APC* corresponding to C'. But when *DI* is greater than $100, *C* is higher than C'. Thus, for *DI* greater than $100, the *APC*

corresponding to *C* is greater than the *APC* corresponding to C'.

(e)

C''
$ 90
105
120
135
150

(g) If the *MPC* changes, the slope will change. If the *APC* changes and the *MPC* does not, the slope will not change, but the function will shift either upward or downward.

4. (a)

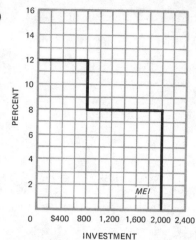

INVESTMENT
Firm A

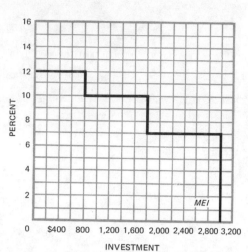

INVESTMENT
Firm B

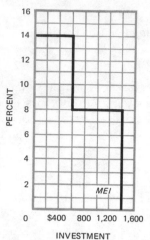

INVESTMENT
Firm C

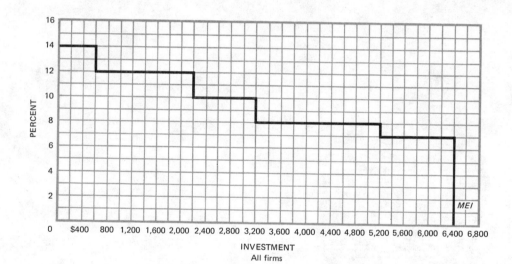

INVESTMENT
All firms

(b) demand curve
total private investment demand curve

(c)
Firm A	$0
Firm B	0
Firm C	0
Total	0

(d)
Firm A	$ 0
Firm B	0
Firm C	600
Total	600

(e)
Firm A	$ 800
Firm B	800
Firm C	600
Total	2,200

(f)
Firm A	$2,000
Firm B	3,000
Firm C	1,400
Total	6,400

(g) less

5. (a) +
(b) +
(c) –
(d) +
(e) 0

Answers to True–False Questions

1.	F	7.	T	13.	F
2.	F	8.	T	14.	T
3.	F	9.	F	15.	T
4.	T	10.	F	16.	T
5.	F	11.	F	17.	F
6.	F	12.	F	18.	T

Answers to Multiple-Choice Questions

1.	c	7.	b	13.	b
2.	c	8.	c	14.	b
3.	a	9.	c	15.	a
4.	a	10.	e	16.	a
5.	d	11.	d	17.	e
6.	e	12.	a		

CHAPTER 10

Income and Employment Determination

CHAPTER ORIENTATION

This chapter develops and explains the following concepts:

The simple theory of income determination, in which income and employment are shown to be determined by the level of aggregate demand.

The idea that planned investment includes only planned inventory changes, whereas realized investment includes actual inventory changes, whether planned or not.

The multiplier principle, which shows how an initial change in aggregate demand has a "multiplied" effect on output and income, the size of the effect being measured by $1/MPS$ or $1/(1 - MPC)$.

The paradox of thrift, which indicates that an attempt by households to save more will not only reduce income and employment but might even lead to a reduction in actual saving.

Inflationary and deflationary gaps, which measure the difference between full-employment output and the level of aggregate demand that would exist at that level of output.

FILL-IN QUESTIONS

Complete the following sentences. (Answers are given at the end of the chapter.)

1. Additions to plant, equipment, and inventories, whether planned or unplanned, are called _____ investment.

2. When we include in investment only *planned* inventory changes, we are speaking of _____ investment.

3. The ratio of the change in income which results from a given change in investment to that change in investment is called _____ .

4. When everyone in society attempts to save more but ends up saving less, the result is called _____ _____ .

5. When investment increases with rising levels of income, investment is said to be _____ .

6. The amount by which aggregate demand exceeds aggregate supply at full employment is called the _____ _____ .

7. The amount by which aggregate demand falls short of aggregate supply at full employment is called the

_____.

PROBLEMS

(Answers are given at the end of the chapter.)

1. Assume that the economy is initially in equilibrium with planned investment equal to *I*, as shown in the graph.

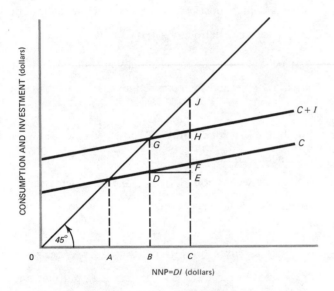

(a) The equilibrium level of income is _____ .

(b) The *MPC* equals the ratio of line segment _____ to line segment _____ .

(c) The *APC* at income level *OB* equals the ratio of line segment _____ to line segment _____ .

(d) If *OC* is the full-employment level of NNP and planned investment equals *I*, a(n) _____ gap exists equal to line segment _____ .

(e) In equilibrium, saving can be measured by line segment _____ .

(f) If income were actually at level *OC*, the unintended change in business inventories could be measured by line segment _____ .

2. (a) Fill in the last three columns of the table.

NNP = DI	C	Planned I	S	Aggregate demand	Unplanned inventory change
$100	$ 80	$50	$_____	$_____	$_____
120	90	50	_____	_____	_____
140	100	50	_____	_____	_____
160	110	50	_____	_____	_____
180	120	50	_____	_____	_____

(b) At NNP $120, aggregate demand is (more than/equal to/less than) _____ aggregate output, planned saving is (more than/equal to/less than) _____ intended investment, and inventories are (being unintentionally depleted/not changing unintentionally/being unintentionally accumulated) _____

_____

_____.

Thus, NNP will tend to (decrease/stay the same/increase) _____ .

(c) At NNP $180, aggregate demand is (more than/equal to/less than) _____ aggregate output, planned saving is (more than/equal to/less than) _____ intended investment, and inventories are (being unintentionally depleted/not changing unintentionally/being unintentionally accumulated) _____

_____

_____.

Thus, NNP will tend to (decrease/stay the same/increase) _____ .

(d) The equilibrium level of income is $ _____ . At this level, planned saving is (more than/equal to/less than) _____ intended investment, and inventories are (being unintentionally depleted/not changing unintentionally/being unintentionally accumulated) _____

_____

_____ . Thus, NNP will tend to

(decrease/stay the same/increase) _____

_____ .

3. Consider the following three consumption–income relationships.

NNP = DI	C	C'	C"
$100	$120	$110	$110
120	130	125	120
140	140	140	130
160	150	155	140
180	160	170	150

(a) Draw these three propensities to consume in the space provided (labeling them as above).

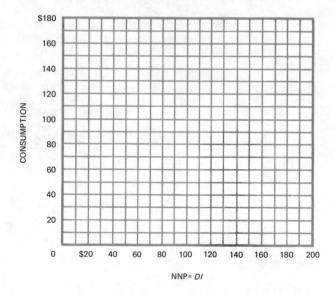

(b) From this graph we can see that consumption

functions _____ and _____ have the same *MPC*s.

(c) At income level $ _____, consumption functions C and C' have the same *APC*s.

(d) Assume that equilibrium income is $160. If the prevailing propensity to consume is C, planned investment

must be $ _____ ; if it is C', planned investment must be $ _____ ; and if it is $C"$, planned investment must be $ _____ .

(e) Assume that planned investment is $10 and the full-employment level of income is $160. The propensity to consume that must prevail if there is a deflationary gap is ($C/C'/C"$) _____ ; that which must prevail if there is an inflationary gap is ($C/C'/C"$) _____ , and that which must prevail if there is neither an inflationary nor a deflationary gap is ($C/C'/C"$) _____ .

4. Assume that the economy is initially in equilibrium with the $MPC = \frac{3}{4}$, and then planned investment increases by $80.

(a) In the first round, this will cause aggregate output and income to rise by $ _____ .

(b) In the second round, $ _____ of this increased income will be spent on

_____ , thus causing

business inventories to _____ . Seeing this,

firms will _____ output, thus

generating $ _____ of additional income and output. Of this, households will spend $ _____ on

_____ , again causing

business inventories to _____ . Thus, firms

will _____ output again.

(c) This process will continue until income has increased

by $ _____ . When this has happened, aggregate

_____ will equal aggregate output, and

planned _____ will

equal saving.

5. Assume that the economy is initially in equilibrium and then planned investment increases by $1,000. Show in the table the successive rounds of income generation that will result. Assume that the MPC is $\frac{1}{2}$.

Round	Increase in income	Increase in consumption	Increase in saving
(Investment increases by $1,000)			
1	$_____	$_____	$_____
2	_____	_____	_____
3	_____	_____	_____
4	_____	_____	_____
All other	_____	_____	_____
Total	_____	_____	_____

6. Assume that an economy without a government or international sector is in equilibrium with NNP = $1,000, planned investment = $200, and the $MPC = \frac{3}{4}$.

   (a) Saving is $ _____ .

   (b) The APC is _____ .

   (c) If planned investment increases to $300, NNP will rise to $ _____ .

   (d) If the MPC does not change but (with investment = $200) consumption changes to $700, the new equilibrium level of NNP will be $ _____ .

SELF-TEST: TRUE-FALSE QUESTIONS

Circle T if the statement is true, F if it is false. (Answers are given at the end of the chapter.)

T F 1. Aggregate supply and the level of employment tend to be directly related.

T F 2. By assuming that planned investment does not change with income, we are, in fact, assuming that planned investment is constant over time.

T F 3. For NNP to be at equilibrium, aggregate demand must equal aggregate supply.

T F 4. For NNP to be at equilibrium, planned saving must equal planned investment.

T F 5. If NNP is above the equilibrium level, planned saving exceeds planned investment and inventories are unintentionally accumulating.

T F 6. If income is below the equilibrium level, aggregate demand must exceed total output.

T F 7. The multiplier process refers to the idea that if consumption increases, then saving will also increase, releasing resources for new investment and thereby creating new jobs and income.

T F 8. If investment in plant and equipment increases, setting off a multiplier process, and during this process firms do not attempt to build up their inventories as income increases, then when the economy reaches its new equilibrium, inventories will be lower than they were originally.

T F 9. The greater the MPC, the smaller the multiplier.

T F 10. The greater the MPC, the greater the slope of the propensity to consume.

T F 11. The size of the multiplier does not depend on the change in investment.

T F 12. A shift in any of the components of aggregate demand will induce a multiplier response.

T F 13. An increase in the propensity to save need not result in greater saving in the aggregate.

T F 14. Inflationary and deflationary gaps refer to the difference between actual output and full-employment output.

SELF-TEST: MULTIPLE-CHOICE QUESTIONS

Circle the letter that corresponds to the best answer. (Answers are given at the end of the chapter.)

1. When planned saving equals planned investment (if there is no government and no international sector):
   (a) NNP is in equilibrium.
   (b) Consumption plus planned investment equals NNP.
   (c) Aggregate supply equals aggregate demand.
   (d) There are no unplanned inventory changes.
   (e) All of the above.

2. When aggregate supply exceeds aggregate demand:
   (a) Unemployment exists.
   (b) Business inventories are unintentionally accumulating.
   (c) People must be saving more than they had planned to.
   (d) Prices must be rising.
   (e) Prices must be falling.

3. The size of the multiplier:
   (a) Depends on the level of investment spending.
   (b) Is greater, the greater the *MPC.*
   (c) Is greater, the smaller the *MPC.*
   (d) Varies with the *APS.*
   (e) Is greater, the greater the *APC.*

4. The reason that an increase in demand leads to a greater increase in equilibrium NNP is that:
   (a) As firms increase output to meet demand, income increases, and this leads to induced consumption spending.
   (b) In order to produce more, business firms must increase their investment spending.
   (c) As output increases, prices rise, and this further raises NNP.
   (d) As output increases, people decrease their saving, thereby giving demand an added boost via consumption.
   (e) As output increases, the *MPC* rises.

5. If consumption is $300, planned investment is $200, current output is $400, and full-employment output is $600 (assuming no government and no foreign sector):
   (a) There is a deflationary gap of $200.
   (b) There is an inflationary gap of $200.
   (c) There is a deflationary gap of $100.
   (d) There is an inflationary gap of $100.
   (e) There is not sufficient information to determine whether or not there is an inflationary or deflationary gap.

6. If aggregate demand increases, but firms, instead of increasing production, work off excess inventories:
   (a) Real NNP will rise but prices will fall.
   (b) Real NNP will rise and prices will rise.
   (c) Real NNP will fall and prices will fall.
   (d) Real NNP will fall and prices will rise.
   (e) Real NNP will not change until firms change the level of production.

7. If people plan to save more, they will actually save less if:
   (a) The *MPC* is greater than $\frac{1}{2}$.
   (b) The *MPC* is less than $\frac{1}{2}$.
   (c) Planned investment increases at the same time.
   (d) Planned investment varies directly with the level of income.
   (e) Income taxes are progressive.

At this point you should be able to do all of the following:

1. Define all of the technical terms and concepts listed at the end of the chapter in the text.

2. Describe the relationship between aggregate supply and employment.

3. Explain what is meant by equilibrium output and employment.

4. Graph the relationship between aggregate supply (NNP) and aggregate demand, and between saving and investment, given the propensity to consume and the level of planned net investment.

5. Identify the equilibrium level of output on the graphs, and explain why this is an equilibrium.

6. State the conditions under which business firms have unplanned inventory accumulations and decumulations.

7. Explain why planned investment may not equal actual investment.

8. Explain why planned investment may not equal saving, but realized investment must equal saving.

9. Explain why changes in net investment have a multiplied effect on income and output.

10. Illustrate the multiplier principle graphically.

11. Calculate the size of the multiplier, given either the *MPC* or the *MPS.*

12. Describe the conditions under which an attempt on the part of all households to save more will result in their saving less, and explain why this is so.

13. Measure and illustrate graphically inflationary and deflationary gaps, given aggregate demand and the full-employment level of output.

QUESTIONS TO THINK ABOUT

1. A dynamic economy such as ours is never in equilibrium. Why, then, is this concept of importance for understanding the real world?

2. Why is it important for the president of the United States to keep in mind the multiplier principle when he is planning policy?

3. A change in investment of $100 and a change in consumption of $100 both have the same effect on equilibrium NNP, other things being equal. How can this be so when investment adds to productive capacity whereas consumption does not?

4. How long it takes the multiplier process to work itself out when demand changes depends on how quickly business firms' production decisions respond to changed sales and how quickly households' consumption decisions respond to changed income. What types of factors might influence the speed of these responses?

5. "Confidence is probably the major factor influencing the level of business activity." Do you agree?

Answers to Fill-in Questions

1. realized

2. planned

3. the multiplier

4. the paradox of thrift

5. induced

6. inflationary gap

7. deflationary gap

Answers to Problems

1. (a) *OB*
   (b) *EF*
      DE
   (c) *BD*
      OB
   (d) deflationary
      HJ
   (e) *DG*
   (f) *HJ* (note that this is the amount by which aggregate supply exceeds aggregate demand)

2. (a)

S	Aggregate demand	Unplanned inventory change
$20	$130	−$30
30	140	− 20
40	150	− 10
50	160	0
60	170	+ 10

   (b) more than
      less than
      being unintentionally depleted
      increase
   (c) less than
      more than
      being unintentionally accumulated
      decrease
   (d) $160
      equal to
      not changing unintentionally
      stay the same

3. (a)

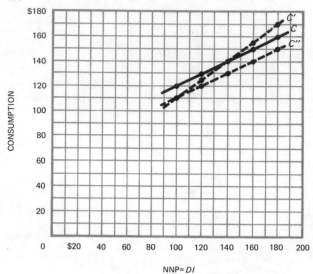

NNP=*DI*

   (b) *C*
      C″
   (c) $140
   (d) $10
      $5
      $20
   (e) *C″*
      C′
      C

4. (a) $80
   (b) $60
      consumption
      fall
      increase
      $60
      $45
      consumption
      fall
      increase
   (c) $320
      demand
      investment

5.

Round	Increase in income	Increase in consumption	Increase in saving
1	$1,000	$ 500	$ 500
2	500	250	250
3	250	125	125
4	125	62.50	62.50
All other	125	62.50	62.50
Total	2,000	1,000	1,000

6. (a) $200   (c) $1,400
 (b) 0.8   (d) $600

10. T   12. T   14. F
11. T   13. T

Answers to True–False Questions

1. T   4. T   7. F
2. F   5. T   8. T
3. T   6. T   9. F

Answers to Multiple-Choice Questions

1. e   4. a   6. e
2. b   5. e   7. d
3. b

CHAPTER 11

Fiscal Policy for Economic Efficiency and Stability

CHAPTER ORIENTATION

This chapter develops and explains the following concepts:

How government spending and taxing policies affect aggregate demand.

How automatic stabilizers modify fluctuations in income, output, employment, and prices.

The sources of funds available to the government and the different uses to which these funds may be put in the exercise of discretionary fiscal policy.

Fiscal drag and the different types of fiscal dividends which may be used to offset it.

Different types of budget policies and their influence on the national debt.

Burdens and benefits arising out of the existence of a national debt.

FILL-IN QUESTIONS

Complete the following sentences. (Answers are given at the end of the chapter.)

1. The act that requires the federal government to use its fiscal powers of taxing and spending to stimulate full employment and economic growth is called _____ _____ _____.

2. The principle that says that if G and T are increased or decreased simultaneously by the same amount, NNP will increase or decrease by that amount is called _____ _____ _____.

3. Deliberate actions by the government in its spending and taxing activities to achieve price stability, to help dampen the swings of business cycles, and to bring the nation's output and employment to desired levels are called _____.

4. Factors that operate to cushion cyclical swings in economic activity without active changes in government policy are called _____ _____.

5. Government-sponsored construction or development projects that would not ordinarily be undertaken by the private sector of the economy are called _____ ____ _____.

6. The automatic and more rapid increases in tax revenues relative to expenditures that a growing economy experiences are called _____.

7. The estimate of annual government expenditures and revenues that would occur if the economy were operating at full employment is called the _____ _____.

8. A budget that is balanced for a 12-month period is called a(n) _____ _____.

9. A budget that is balanced over the course of the business cycle is called a(n) _____ _____.

10. The philosophy which holds that the government should pursue whatever fiscal measures are needed to achieve noninflationary full employment and economic growth without regard to budget balancing per se is called _____ _____.

PROBLEMS

(Answers are given at the end of the chapter.)

1. On the basis of the information given, answer the following questions.

NNP	DI	C	I	G
$1,000	$ 900	$ 650	$350	$100
1,200	1,100	750	350	100
1,400	1,300	850	350	100
1,600	1,500	950	350	100
1,800	1,700	1,050	350	100

(a) Equilibrium will occur when NNP is $ _____.

(b) The *MPC* is _____.

(c) The multiplier is _____.

(d) If government purchases of goods and services were to increase to $200, equilibrium NNP would rise to $ _____.

(e) As income is rising because of the change in government demand, fiscal drag (will/will not) _____ _____ occur.

2. Refer to the table given in Problem 1.

(a) In the space below draw the relationship between consumption and NNP and label it *C*. The slope of the consumption function is _____.

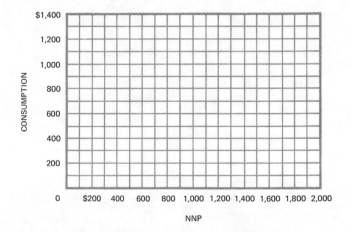

(b) Assume now that taxes are increased by $100 at each level of NNP and that the *MPC* remains the same. Draw the new consumption function and label it *C'*.

(c) Government spending would have to increase by $ _____ to offset the decrease in aggregate demand caused by the tax increase.

3. Assume that economists have estimated what tax receipts, government purchases of goods and services, and unemployment would be for a particular economy at different levels of NNP. These estimates are presented in the table.

NNP	Estimated tax receipts	Estimated government purchases of goods and services	Estimated unemployment (%)
$1,000	$150	$300	7
1,200	200	300	5
1,400	275	300	4
1,600	375	300	3

(a) This economy appears to have a (progressive/neutral/regressive) _____ tax structure.

(b) If 4 percent unemployment is considered to be full employment, the full-employment (surplus/deficit) _____ is $ _____ .

(c) If 3 percent unemployment is considered to be full employment, the full-employment (surplus/deficit) _____ is $ _____ .

(d) If NNP were to grow from $1,000 to $1,600, fiscal drag would amount to $ _____ .

SELF-TEST: TRUE-FALSE QUESTIONS

Circle T if the statement is true, F if it is false. (Answers are given at the end of the chapter.)

T F 1. With regard to their influence on aggregate demand, $1 of consumption demand is equivalent to $1 of government demand for goods and services.

T F 2. If investment demand increases by $100 and government demand for goods and services decreases by $100, other things remaining the same, NNP will rise by $100.

T F 3. If taxes are increased by $100, consumption will decrease by an amount that depends on the *MPC*.

T F 4. If taxes are increased by $100 and government purchases of goods and services are also increased by $100, NNP will increase by an amount that depends on the *MPC*.

T F 5. An increase in government spending, other things remaining the same, will ultimately lead to an increase in the amount that people save.

T F 6. A fiscal policy of reducing taxes and government purchases of goods and services by the same amount would be anti-inflationary.

T F 7. If corporations paid out all earnings in the form of dividends, corporate dividend policy would not provide automatic stabilization.

T F 8. If the *MPC* of upper-income groups is lower than the *MPC* of lower-income groups, taxing money away from the rich and distributing it to the poor would raise aggregate demand.

T F 9. If government spending is increased by $100, the result will probably be more expansionary if the $100 is financed by taxes than if it is financed by borrowing.

T F 10. Financing government expenditures by printing new money is always inflationary.

T F 11. An increase of transfer expenditures of $1 will always have the same effect on aggregate demand as an increase of government spending of the same amount.

T F 12. Because state and local government budgets tend to be procyclical, there is reduced need for countercyclical fiscal policy at the federal level.

T F 13. The more steeply progressive an economy's tax structure, the greater fiscal drag will be, other things being equal.

T F 14. If the government is running a surplus when the economy is in a recession, its fiscal policy is "correct" from the point of view of economic stabilization.

T F 15. If an economy is in a recession and its full-employment surplus exceeds its actual surplus, its actual surplus should be increased by raising taxes and lowering spending.

T F 16. It would be inappropriate to declare a fiscal dividend to take care of fiscal drag in an economy experiencing demand inflation.

T F 17. A fiscal dividend of $1 has the same effect on aggregate demand whether it is in the form of a tax cut or a spending increase.

T F 18. An annually balanced budget tends, in fact, to accentuate cyclical swings.

T F 19. If the budget is balanced cyclically, there will be no change in the national debt.

T F 20. Functional finance will normally yield a high-employment balanced budget.

T F 21. The burden of increasing the public debt tends to be greater in inflationary periods than in periods of unemployment, other things remaining the same.

T F 22. To the extent that the public debt is held by poor widows and orphans, the transfer payments' burden of the debt will be small or even negative.

SELF-TEST: MULTIPLE-CHOICE QUESTIONS

Circle the letter that corresponds to the best answer. (Answers are given at the end of the chapter.)

1. If government spending decreases by $100, taxes do not change, and the $MPC = \frac{2}{3}$, NNP will:
   (a) Increase by $100.
   (b) Increase by $200.
   (c) Increase by $300.
   (d) Decrease by $300.
   (e) Decrease by $100.

2. NNP will increase if:
   (a) Taxes are increased by $1 and government spending is increased by $1 × *MPC*.
   (b) Taxes are increased by $1 and government spending is reduced by $1.
   (c) Taxes are reduced by $1 and government spending is reduced by $1 × *MPC*.
   (d) Taxes are increased by $1 × *MPC* and government spending is increased by $1.
   (e) Taxes are increased by $1 × *MPC* and government spending is reduced by $1 × *MPC*.

3. If taxes are increased by $1:
   (a) Government spending will increase by $1.
   (b) Government spending will increase by $1 × *MPC*.
   (c) Consumption at each level of NNP will fall by $1.
   (d) Consumption at each level of NNP will fall by $1 × *MPC*.
   (e) There is no reason to believe that any component of aggregate demand will change.

4. A reduction in government purchases of goods and services by $1:
   (a) Will be neutralized in its effect on NNP by a reduction in taxes of the same amount.
   (b) Will ultimately lead to decrease in NNP of $1 × 1/*MPS*, other things remaining the same.
   (c) Will ultimately lead to an increase in personal saving of $1 × *MPS*.
   (d) Will ultimately lead to a decrease in the public debt of $1.
   (e) Will lead to an increase in private purchases of $1.

5. By "built-in" stabilizers, we mean:
   (a) Any factors that automatically tend to reduce cyclical fluctuations in economic activity.
   (b) Any factors that cause aggregate demand to change procyclically.
   (c) Any factors that cause unemployment to change procyclically.
   (d) Any factors that cause the rate of growth to increase.
   (e) Any factors that reduce fluctuations in NNP relative to fluctuations in employment and prices.

6. Which of the following is *not* an example of an automatic stabilizer?
   (a) Unemployment taxes.
   (b) Corporation dividend policy.
   (c) A progressive tax system.
   (d) Unemployment benefits.
   (e) Fiscal dividends.

7. Public works expenditures:
   (a) Are relatively inflexible with regard to timing.
   (b) Tend to stimulate the capital goods and construction industries, where unemployment is usually heavy during a recession.
   (c) Tend to provide socially useful goods.
   (d) Sometimes compete with and thereby discourage private investment in certain areas.
   (e) All of the above.

8. By fiscal drag we mean the tendency for:
   (a) Tax revenues to increase relative to expenditures in an expanding economy.
   (b) Congress to cut spending as full employment is reached.
   (c) State and local governments to cut spending during recessions.
   (d) Congress to reduce taxes as income rises.
   (e) Congress to reduce the debt ceiling as the economy approaches full employment.

9. A full-employment budget surplus implies that:
   (a) Tax rates are too low.
   (b) Tax rates are too high.
   (c) Government spending is too high.
   (d) Government spending is too high in relation to tax rates.
   (e) If the economy were at full employment, tax revenues would exceed government expenditures.

10. Functional finance:
    (a) Is consistent with the philosophy of annually balanced budgets.
    (b) Views the budget as a tool of stabilization policy.

(c) Always rules out tax increases when the economy is in a recession.

(d) Always rules out increases in government purchases of goods and services when there is inflation.

(e) Rules out fiscal dividends to offset fiscal drag.

11. A full-employment balanced budget:

(a) Tends to produce a balanced budget over the business cycle.

(b) Relies on automatic stabilizers to keep the economy at full employment.

(c) Sets government expenditures at a level consistent with social wants.

(d) Sets tax rates in relation to the level of government expenditures so as to provide a balanced budget or a moderate surplus at full employment.

(e) All of the above.

12. Creation of public debt will be burdensome if:

(a) It creates inflation.

(b) It is held by foreigners.

(c) It results in the net using up of capital goods.

(d) It requires the poor to be taxed to pay interest on the debt which is held by the rich.

(e) All of the above.

13. Which of the following should *not* influence the rate at which the national debt is allowed to grow?

(a) The fear of bankruptcy.

(b) The rate of growth of GNP.

(c) The willingness of the public to pay higher taxes.

(d) The amount of interest that will have to be paid on the debt in relation to GNP over time.

(e) The taxable capacity of a nation.

CHECKPOINT: LEARNING OBJECTIVES

At this point you should be able to do all of the following:

1. Define all of the technical terms and concepts listed at the end of the chapter in the text.

2. Explain and show graphically how government expenditures influence aggregate demand and equilibrium NNP.

3. Explain why a change in government spending has a multiplied effect on NNP just as a change in investment does.

4. State how much government spending should be increased to reach full employment if NNP is below the full-employment level, given either the deflationary gap or the difference between actual and full-employment NNP and the *MPC.*

5. Explain why and by how much a given change in taxes affects aggregate demand, and be able to show this graphically.

6. Explain why increasing or decreasing G and T by the same amount increases or decreases NNP by that amount.

7. Describe the different combinations of changes in G and T which may be used to close inflationary and deflationary gaps.

8. Explain why each of the following is or has been an atuomatic stabilizer:

(a) Tax receipts.

(b) Unemployment taxes and benefits.

(c) Agricultural price supports.

(d) Corporate dividend policy.

9. Explain whether or not the effect on NNP of a tax change depends on the type of tax that is being changed.

10. Explain how raising revenues through each of the following is likely to affect the economy:

(a) Sales of government bonds.

(b) Printing money.

11. Explain how transfer expenditures are likely to affect income and employment.

12. Discuss the advantages and disadvantages of using public works expenditures for stabilization purposes.

13. Discuss each of the following problems associated with fiscal policy:

(a) Timing.

(b) Political and public acceptance.

(c) Federal versus state and local fiscal policies.

(d) Dovetailing government and private investment.

14. Explain why the full-employment budget more accurately reflects the impact of government surpluses and deficits on the economy than does the actual or current budget.

15. Discuss the advantages and disadvantages, if any, of each of the following budget policies:

(a) Annually balanced budgets.

(b) Cyclically balanced budgets.

(c) Functional finance.

(d) Full-employment balanced budgets.

16. Discuss whether the national debt:

(a) Endangers national credit.

(b) Burdens future generations.

17. Explain what is meant by each of the following burdens of the debt:

(a) External-debt burden.

(b) Capital-consumption burden.

(c) Inflationary burden.

(d) Transfer-payments burden.

(e) Debt-management burden.

18. Describe the two benefits of a public debt.

19. Discuss whether or not the public debt should be allowed to grow without limit.

QUESTIONS TO THINK ABOUT

1. Would discretionary fiscal policy work better if discretion were in the hands of the executive rather than the legislative branch of government?

2. What do you suppose would happen to the size of the multiplier if the tax system were made more progressive?

3. The federal government can exert a given influence on the level of aggregate demand through an infinite number of *combinations* of tax and spending policies. But from the point of view of economic growth the different combinations will have different effects. Why?

4. "Built-in stabilizers apparently have not worked since we have not experienced anything approaching economic stability." Do you agree?

5. "If when people purchase government bonds they decrease their saving and leave their consumption the same, it would be no more inflationary for the government to finance its expenditures by printing new money than by borrowing." Is this true?

6. What is the point to public works expenditures if they result in some people digging holes and others filling them up, as sometimes appeared to be the case during the Great Depression?

7. To compare the impact of the federal government on the economy in two different years, the full-employment budgets will be more useful than the actual budgets. Why?

8. "It is likely that if burdens and benefits could be measured, the benefits of our national debt would exceed the burdens imposed by it." Do you agree?

ANSWERS

Answers to Fill-in Questions

1. the Employment Act of 1946
2. the balanced-budget multiplier principle
3. fiscal policy
4. automatic or "built-in" stabilizers
5. public works
6. fiscal drag
7. full-employment budget
8. annually balanced budget
9. cyclically balanced budget
10. functional finance

Answers to Problems

1. (a) $1,200
   (b) $\frac{1}{2}$
   (c) 2
   (d) $1,400
   (e) will not (because taxes are assumed to be $100 regardless of the level of NNP)

2. (a), (b)

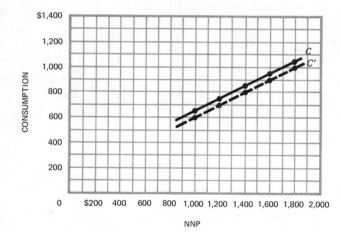

   (a) $\frac{1}{2}$
   (c) $50
3. (a) progressive
   (b) deficit
      $25
   (c) surplus
      $75
   (d) $225

Answers to True–False Questions

1.	T	12.	F
2.	F	13.	T
3.	T	14.	F
4.	F	15.	F
5.	T	16.	T
6.	T	17.	F
7.	T	18.	T
8.	T	19.	F
9.	F	20.	F
10.	F	21.	T
11.	F	22.	T

Answers to Multiple-Choice Questions

1.	d	6.	e	10.	b
2.	d	7.	e	11.	e
3.	d	8.	a	12.	e
4.	b	9.	e	13.	a
5.	a				

PART 3

Money, Banking, and Monetary Policy: The Fiscal–Monetary Mix

CHAPTER 12

Our Monetary and Banking System

CHAPTER ORIENTATION

This chapter develops and explains the following concepts:

The definition of money and near-monies, and the nature of several different monetary standards.

Different types of credit instruments and the functions of credit in our economy.

The nature of the money and capital markets in which different types of credit and equity instruments are traded.

Different types of financial intermediaries, and how they serve the money and capital markets.

The objectives, organization, and functions of the Federal Reserve System.

The structure and regulation of our dual-banking system.

FILL-IN QUESTIONS

Complete the following sentences. (Answers are given at the end of the chapter.)

1. The _____ , according to most economists, consists of currency, coin, and demand deposits.

2. Money in a bank account which the bank promises to pay upon request is called a _____ .

   An account for which the bank can require advance notice of withdrawal is called a _____ .

3. Assets whose values are known in terms of money and can easily be converted into money are called _____ .

4. One person's promise to pay another a specified sum of money by a given date is called a _____ .

5. An agreement to pay a specified sum of money either at a future date or periodically over the course of the loan, during which time a fixed rate of interest may be paid on certain dates, is called a _____ .

6. A market in which short-term credit instruments are bought and sold is called a _____.

One in which long-term financial instruments such as bonds, stock, and mortgages are bought and sold is called a

_____ .

7. Institutions that act as middlemen between lenders and borrowers are called _____

_____ .

8. The only type of institution that can make loans by creating demand deposits and retire loans by canceling demand deposits is the _____ .

9. The central bank of the United States is called the

_____ .

10. Commercial banks that are chartered by the federal government are called _____ banks. All other commercial banks are called _____ banks and are charted by _____

_____ .

11. The federal agency that insures bank deposits against loss due to bank failure is called the _____

_____ .

SELF-TEST: TRUE–FALSE QUESTIONS

Circle T if the statement is true, F if it is false. (Answers are given at the end of the chapter.)

T F 1. Many economists exclude time deposits from the money supply because they are not directly "spendable."

T F 2. Currency consists of paper money and demand deposits.

T F 3. A major problem with the gold coin standard is that it ties the domestic money supply to the amount of gold that a country has.

T F 4. It is not possible for a country to be on one monetary standard for domestic purposes and a different monetary standard for international purposes.

T F 5. A major problem with a bimetallic monetary standard is that, in fact, only one metal tends to circulate and the other tends to be hoarded or melted down.

T F 6. Under an inconvertible paper standard, a nation's money is always defined in terms of paper, not in terms of a metal or any other commodity.

T F 7. The value of money is defined in terms of its purchasing power.

T F 8. The greater the amount of credit outstanding in an economy, the greater the amount of debt that must exist.

T F 9. If credit did not exist, investing would have to be done by savers, and vice versa.

T F 10. The capital market is the place where firms buy capital in the form of plant and equipment.

T F 11. A major function performed by the money market is financing the short-term needs of business and the federal government.

T F 12. Among the reasons for the establishment of the Federal Reserve System in 1913 was to create a means whereby the money supply could be expanded and contracted according to the needs of the economy.

T F 13. The primary responsibility of the Federal Reserve is to print money.

T F 14. National banks need not be members of the Federal Reserve System.

T F 15. Federal Reserve banks technically are owned by member banks, but their profits go largely to the U.S. Treasury.

T F 16. Governors of the Federal Reserve System are all members of the Open Market Committee, but not all members of the Open Market Committee are governors.

T F 17. Only member banks can be insured by the FDIC.

T F 18. Almost all banks in the United States are supervised by at least two government agencies.

Circle the letter that corresponds to the best answer.
(Answers are given at the end of the chapter.)

1. Money does *not* function as a:
   (a) Medium of exchange.
   (b) Hedge against inflation.
   (c) Store of value.
   (d) Standard of deferred payments.
   (e) Measure of value.

2. Which of the following is *not* part of the U.S. money supply?
   (a) A $10 bill.
   (b) A $10 demand deposit.
   (c) A $10 government bond.
   (d) Forty quarters.
   (e) Five $2 bills.

3. Which of the following is *not* essential under the gold standard?
   (a) Free coinage of gold.
   (b) Free movement of gold into and out of the country.
   (c) Existence of a mint ratio between gold and other precious metals.
   (d) Gold coins being legal tender.
   (e) The national currency defined in terms of a fixed weight of gold.

4. Under the gold bullion standard:
   (a) Gold does not circulate.
   (b) Gold is held in the form of coins.
   (c) Gold is not available for industrial use.
   (d) Gold is not used to settle international transactions.
   (e) The price of gold is determined by the quantity in circulation.

5. If a country is on a bimetallic standard with a mint ratio (gold to silver) of 1:5, then:
   (a) If the market price of gold is more than five times the market price of silver, gold will go out of circulation.
   (b) If the market price of gold is more than five times the market price of silver, silver will go out of circulation.
   (c) The amount of each metal in circulation is unaffected by the ratio of their market prices.
   (d) The market prices of gold and silver cannot deviate from the ratio 1:5.
   (e) If the market price ratio is 1:5, both metals will go out of circulation.

6. Which of the following is *not* an example of a credit instrument?
   (a) An IOU.
   (b) A bond.
   (c) A share of stock.
   (d) A draft.
   (e) A banker's acceptance.

7. During most of the 1930s, the United States was on:
   (a) An inconvertible paper standard domestically and a gold bullion standard internationally.
   (b) A gold bullion standard domestically and a gold standard internationally.
   (c) A gold standard domestically and an inconvertible paper standard internationally.
   (d) A gold standard domestically and a gold bullion standard internationally.
   (e) An inconvertible paper standard both domestically and internationally.

8. Which of the following instruments would *not* be traded in the capital market?
   (a) Municipal bonds.
   (b) Corporate bonds.
   (c) Mortgages.
   (d) Corporate stock.
   (e) U.S. Treasury bills.

9. Which of the following would *not* be an example of a financial intermediary?
   (a) A commercial bank.
   (b) A mutual savings bank.
   (c) A savings and loan association.
   (d) A credit union.
   (e) All of the above are financial intermediaries.

10. Which of the following is *not* a part of the Federal Reserve System?
    (a) The Federal Advisory Council.
    (b) The Open Market Committee.
    (c) The Board of Governors.
    (d) All state banks.
    (e) Federal Reserve Banks.

11. Which of the following is *not* true of banks which are members of the Federal Reserve System?
    (a) They must pay a membership tax as a percent of their profit to the U.S. Treasury.
    (b) They must subscribe to the capital stock of their district Federal Reserve bank.
    (c) They must keep reserves behind their demand deposit liabilities.
    (d) They must keep their reserves in the form of vault cash and/or deposits in their district Federal Reserve Bank.

(e) They may but need not borrow from the Federal Reserve.

12. Which of the following is *not* true of credit?
    (a) It channels saving into investment.
    (b) It involves the creation of short-term but not long-term debt instruments.
    (c) It permits the time pattern of consumption to be changed.
    (d) It facilitates trade.
    (e) It permits the existence of financial markets.

CHECKPOINT: LEARNING OBJECTIVES

At this point you should be able to do all of the following:

1. Define all of the technical terms and concepts listed at the end of the chapter in the text.

2. Distinguish among the following:
    (a) The gold coin standard.
    (b) The gold bullion standard.
    (c) The gold exchange standard.
    (d) A bimetallic standard.
    (e) An inconvertible paper standard.
    State the place of each in economic history.

3. Explain what is meant by the value of money and why it is measured by the reciprocal of the price level.

4. Explain the two major functions of credit, and give some examples of short-term and long-term credit instruments.

5. Describe the role of financial intermediaries in the economy, and state the most important difference between commercial banks and other financial institutions.

6. Explain why it is essential for financial institutions to maintain liquidity.

7. Explain why prior to the establishment of the Federal Reserve System, there were recurrent money panics.

8. Describe the organization of the Federal Reserve System and state its primary objective.

9. State the primary privileges and obligations of commercial banks which are members of the Federal Reserve System.

10. State who owns the Federal Reserve banks, and what these banks do with their profits.

11. Describe how members of the Board of Governors are selected, and the primary function of the Board.

12. Describe the membership of the Federal Open Market Committee, and state its chief function.

13. Explain what is meant by our "dual-banking system" and state which supervisory agencies have responsibility for which banks.

QUESTIONS TO THINK ABOUT

1. Economists argue over what should be included in the money supply. Why does it make any difference?

2. Should the quantity of gold a country has influence its decision regarding whether or not to be on the gold standard?

3. Why do you suppose that credit conditions (interest rates, availability, etc.) tend to be the same all over the country at any point in time?

4. What do you think an economy without financial institutions would be like? Would it be very different from ours?

5. Should credit cards be included in the money supply? If so, how would you measure their contribution to the money supply? If not, why not?

ANSWERS

Answers to Fill-in Questions

1. money supply

2. demand deposit
   time deposit

3. near-monies

4. promissory note

5. bond

6. money market
   capital market

7. financial intermediaries

8. commercial bank

9. Federal Reserve System

10. national
    state
    state governments

11. Federal Deposit Insurance
    Corporation

Answers to True–False Question

1.	T	10.	F
2.	F	11.	T
3.	T	12.	T
4.	F	13.	F
5.	T	14.	F
6.	F	15.	T
7.	T	16.	T
8.	T	17.	F
9.	T	18.	T

Answers to Multiple-Choice Questions

1.	b	7.	a
2.	c	8.	e
3.	c	9.	e
4.	a	10.	d
5.	a	11.	a
6.	c	12.	b

CHAPTER 13

Commercial Banking: Money Creation and Portfolio Management

CHAPTER ORIENTATION

This chapter develops and explains the following concepts:

The "goldsmiths' principle," which explains why banks can operate with reserves which are less than their deposit liabilities.

The definition of and relationship among legal reserves, required reserves, and excess reserves.

How the banking system can, when it has excess reserves, engage in a multiple expansion of deposits, and why, when it is deficient in reserves, it must engage in a multiple contraction of deposits.

Bank portfolio management, which involves the selection of asset portfolios which optimize a combination of liquidity, profitability, and safety.

FILL-IN QUESTIONS

Complete the following sentences. (Answers are given at the end of the chapter.)

1. Things of value which any economic entity owns are called its _____. The monetary debts or things of value which it owes to its creditors are called its _____. The difference between the former and the latter is its _____. When these three classes of data are grouped together for analysis and interpretation, the financial statement on which they appear is called a _____.

2. Assets that a bank may lawfully use as reserves against its deposit liabilities are called _____ reserves.

3. The minimum amount that a bank is required by law to keep in the form of legal reserves behind its deposit liabilities is called _____.

4. The quantity of a bank's legal reserves over and above its required reserves is called _____.

5. The reciprocal of the reserve requirement is the expression for the _____

   _____ .

6. _____ is defined as the ease with which an asset can be converted into cash quickly without loss of value in money terms.

7. The difference between what you pay for a bond and what you realize when you redeem or sell it, plus any returns you receive in the interim, expressed in percentage terms is called the _____ .

8. The sum of a bank's legal reserves and its demand deposits at other banks is called _____ reserves.

9. Earning assets of a bank that are readily convertible into cash on short notice without substantial loss are called _____ reserves.

10. Marketable financial obligations issued by state and local governmental authorities are called _____

    _____ .

PROBLEMS

(Answers are given at the end of the chapter.)

1. Record the *changes* which occur in the balance sheet of a bank as an *initial* result of each of the following. Be sure to indicate the direction of change (+ or −) as well as the numerical amount.

   (a) You withdraw $100 from your checking account.

Assets		Liabilities	
Legal reserves	$_____	Deposits	$_____

   (b) A bank makes a loan of $500 in the form of a demand deposit.

Assets		Liabilities	
Legal reserves	$_____	Deposits	$_____
Loans	_____		

   (c) Mr. Aaron writes a $50 check on Bank A and gives it to Mr. Brown, who deposits it in his account in Bank B, and Bank A makes payment on the check.

Bank A

Assets		Liabilities	
Legal reserves	$_____	Deposits	$_____
Loans	_____		

Bank B

Assets		Liabilities	
Legal reserves	$_____	Deposits	$_____
Loans	_____		

   (d) A person writes a $100 check on his account in Bank A to repay a loan outstanding from that bank.

Bank A

Assets		Liabilities	
Legal reserves	$_____	Deposits	$_____
Loans	_____		

2. You are given simplified balance sheets for Bank X and Bank Y. Assume that the reserve requirement is 10 percent.

Bank X

Assets		Liabilities	
Legal reserves	$ 5,000	Demand deposits	$50,000
Loans	47,000	Net worth	2,000

Bank Y

Assets		Liabilities	
Legal reserves	$ 8,000	Demand deposits	$80,000
Loans	75,000	Net worth	3,000

   (a) Assume that a person deposits $100 cash in his demand deposit at Bank X. Record the *changes* that this will make in Bank X's balance sheet.

Bank X

Assets		Liabilities	
Legal reserves	$_____	Demand deposits	$_____
Loans	_____	Net worth	_____

   (b) Bank X's balance sheet will now be:

Bank X

Assets		Liabilities	
Legal reserves	$_____	Demand deposits $_____
Loans	_____	Net worth _____

   (c) Bank X now has required reserves of $ _____ and excess reserves of $ _____ . Assume that it decides to loan out as much as it safely can to a depositor. Record the *changes* that this will make in its balance sheet, assuming that the loan is in the form of a demand deposit.

Bank X

Assets		Liabilities	
Legal reserves	$_____	Demand deposits	$_____
Loans	_____	Net worth	_____

and its balance sheet will now be:

Bank X

Assets		Liabilities	
Legal reserves	$_____	Demand deposits $_____	
Loans	_____	Net worth	_____

(d) Now assume that the person who borrowed the money spends it, the person who receives it deposits it in Bank Y, and Bank X makes payment on the check. Record the *changes* that this makes in the balance sheets of Bank X and Bank Y below.

Bank X

Assets		Liabilities	
Legal reserves	$_____	Demand deposits	$_____
Loans	_____	Net worth	_____

Bank Y

Assets		Liabilities	
Legal reserves	$_____	Demand deposits	$_____
Loans	_____	Net worth	_____

The balance sheets of Bank X and Bank Y now are:

Bank X

Assets		Liabilities	
Legal reserves	$_____	Demand deposits $_____	
Loans	_____	Net worth	_____

Bank Y

Assets		Liabilities	
Legal reserves	$_____	Demand deposits $_____	
Loans	_____	Net worth	_____

Now Bank X has required reserves of $ _____ and excess reserves of $ _____ , and Bank Y has required reserves of $ _____ and excess reserves of $ _____ .

(e) Assume that Bank Y lends out as much as it safely can. It will lend out $ _____ . When it makes this loan, its required reserves will _____ by $ _____ , and its excess reserves will _____ by $ _____ .

(f) Now assume that the loan recipient writes a check for the amount of the loan and gives it to a person who deposits it in Bank Z. When Bank Y makes payment on the check, its legal reserves will _____ by $ _____ , and its excess reserves will equal $ _____ . The legal reserves of Bank Z will _____ by $ _____ , and its required reserves will _____ by $ _____ . As a result of this transaction, it will have excess reserves of $ _____ .

(g) Ultimately, the original $100 deposit could lead to an expansion of deposits of $ _____ (including the initial deposit).

(h) If when the $100 was originally deposited, Bank X wanted to keep 5 percent in excess reserves, it would have loaned out $ _____ . If each bank in the banking system wanted 5 percent excess reserves, deposits could ultimately increase by $ _____ , including the original $100 deposit.

3. Assume that banks have *no* excess reserves, that the reserve requirement is 20 percent, that somebody withdraws $1,000 from his deposit in Bank A, and that this cash does not reenter the banking system.

(a) Record the *changes* that this makes in Bank A's balance sheet.

Bank A

Assets		Liabilities	
Legal reserves	$_____	Deposits	$_____

(b) Bank A has a reserve deficiency of $ _____ .

(c) Assume that Bank A sells government securities for this amount and that the security purchasers pay with checks drawn on Bank B, which in turn makes payment on these checks. Record these transactions below.

Bank A

Assets		Liabilities	
Legal reserves	$_____	Deposits	$_____
Securities	_____		

Bank B

Assets		Liabilities	
Legal reserves	$_____	Deposits	$_____
Securities	_____		

(d) Now Bank B is deficient in legal reserves and must sell $ _____ of securities, assuming that they are purchased by somebody who has an account in another bank.

(e) Assume that this process continues until no bank is short of legal reserves. The money supply will ultimately contract by $ _____ (including the original $1,000 withdrawal).

SELF-TEST: TRUE–FALSE QUESTIONS

Circle T if the statement is true, F if it is false. (Answers are given at the end of the chapter.)

T F 1. A commercial bank is able to create demand deposits only because any money that it lends, when spent, will automatically be redeposited in it, and it will not, therefore, lose reserves through deposit creation.

T F 2. A commercial bank that is not a monopoly bank cannot safely loan out more than its excess reserves.

T F 3. The amount that a monopoly bank can loan out does not depend on the reserve requirement.

T F 4. When the money supply is being expanded by commercial banks and people do not withdraw cash, legal reserves of the banking system do not change, but required reserves increase and excess reserves decrease.

T F 5. The greater the reserve requirement, the greater the deposit-expansion multiplier.

T F 6. The deposit-expansion multiplier for a monopoly banking system is greater than the deposit-expansion multiplier for a banking system that consists of many independent banks, other things being equal.

T F 7. If in the deposit-expansion process there is a leakage of cash into circulation, legal reserves of the banking system decline, other things remaining the same.

T F 8. If bankers desire to hold excess reserves, then from the point of view of the economy as a whole, this is equivalent to the reserve requirement being higher than in fact it is.

T F 9. If the reserve requirement is 10 percent and banks are deficient in reserves by $100, the money supply will have to contract by at least $1,000.

T F 10. A sound bank must organize its operations so that each of its assets is perfectly safe, perfectly liquid, and has a high yield.

T F 11. Banks keep secondary reserves primarily to provide them with liquidity.

T F 12. One reason that banks hold municipals is that the interest earned on them is exempt from federal taxes.

T F 13. Banks derive a large part of their earnings from dividends which they receive on the shares of corporate stock in their portfolios.

SELF-TEST: MULTIPLE-CHOICE QUESTIONS

Circle the letter that corresponds to the best answer. (Answers are given at the end of the chapter.)

1. If you dig up a $100 bill out of your garden and deposit it in your bank which has a 10 percent legal reserve requirement:
   (a) The bank will have $100 of excess reserves.
   (b) The bank will have $100 of required reserves.
   (c) The bank will have $100 of additional legal reserves.
   (d) The bank will lend out $100.
   (e) The bank will lend out $1,000.

2. One reason that the banking system can engage in multiple-deposit creation is:

(a) People continuously put new reserves into the banking system.

(b) Individual banks never lose reserves when checks are written on them and payment is made.

(c) Banks need keep only a fraction of the value of their deposits in legal reserves and can make loans equal to the rest.

(d) Banks keep savings accounts as well as checking accounts and can loan out all "saved" money as well as money in checking accounts.

(e) Each bank can loan an amount equal to several times its excess reserves.

3. If $1,000 is withdrawn from a bank that has no excess reserves and is subject to a 10 percent reserve requirement, that bank, in order to meet this reserve requirement, should:

(a) Increase its legal reserves by $900.

(b) Increase its legal reserves by $100.

(c) Contract demand deposits by $900.

(d) Contract demand deposits by $100.

(e) Contract demand deposits by $90.

4. Assume that the reserve requirement is 10 percent and that banks want to keep an additional 10 percent of deposits in legal reserves. If the legal reserves of the banking system decrease by $100 and banks had the amount of legal reserves they wanted previously, then demand deposits will ultimately fall by:

(a) $1,000

(b) $2,000

(c) $5,000

(d) $4,000

(e) $500

5. When banks are expanding the money supply, if people withdraw cash and put it in their cookie jars, the deposit-expansion potential will be reduced because:

(a) The leakage of cash is, in effect, a reserve drain.

(b) The leakage of cash reduces loans outstanding by a corresponding amount.

(c) The leakage of cash results in an increase in the reserve requirement.

(d) The leakage of cash reduces people's needs for loans.

(e) The leakage of cash causes bank earnings to fall.

6. If the reserve requirement is 20 percent, all banks are fully loaned up, and a person writes a check for $100 in Bank A which is deposited in Bank B and payment is made on the check, the money supply can expand at most by:

(a) $1,000

(b) $800

(c) $500

(d) $100

(e) $0

7. If the reserve requirement is 10 percent and there are $500 excess reserves in the banking system, the money supply may *not* expand by $5,000 if:

(a) People withdraw cash from their deposits.

(b) Banks want to hold excess reserves.

(c) People do not want to borrow from banks.

(d) Banks do not want to lend, or to buy government securities.

(e) All of the above.

8. The relative liquidity of an asset is associated with:

(a) Its marketability.

(b) Its collateral value.

(c) The contractual conditions under which it is issued.

(d) All of the above.

(e) None of the above.

9. If a bank uses some of its deposits at other banks to buy Treasury bills:

(a) Its primary reserves increase, and its secondary reserves decrease.

(b) Its primary reserves decrease, and its secondary reserves increase.

(c) Its primary reserves increase, and its required reserves decrease.

(d) Its primary reserves decrease, and its excess reserves increase.

(e) Its secondary reserves decrease, and its excess reserves increase.

10. Which of the following assets would you *not* be likely to find in the portfolio of a commercial bank?

(a) Municipals.

(b) Treasury bills.

(c) Shares of corporate stock.

(d) Quasi-governmental securities.

(e) Treasury bonds.

CHECKPOINT: LEARNING OBJECTIVES

At this point you should be able to do all of the following:

1. Define all of the technical terms and concepts listed at the end of the chapter in the text.

2. Explain why banks are able to operate with fractional reserves.

3. Explain how much a bank is able to lend, given the amount

of its legal reserves, its demand deposits, and the reserve requirement.

4. Demonstrate, using balance sheets, how the banking system engages in a multiple-deposit expansion when one bank has excess reserves (assuming that the others are fully loaned up), given the reserve requirement.

5. Calculate the amount by which the banking system's deposits can increase, given the amount of its excess reserves and the reserve requirement.

6. Explain how deposit expansion in a monopoly banking system differs from deposit expansion in a system of many independently owned banks.

7. Explain how each of the following affects the multiple expansion of deposits:
   (a) A leakage of cash into circulation.
   (b) Banks' wanting to keep some excess reserves.
   (c) The unwillingness of banks to lend or businessmen to borrow.

8. Demonstrate, using balance sheets, how the banking system engages in a multiple-deposit contraction when one bank has a reserve deficiency (assuming that the others are fully loaned up), given the reserve requirement.

9. Describe the characteristics of an asset which determine its liquidity.

10. State the three fundamental goals for a bank's portfolio, and explain why they tend to be in conflict.

11. State the purpose of each of the following in a bank's portfolio:
    (a) Primary reserves.
    (b) Secondary reserves.
    (c) Loans.
    (d) Investments.
    Describe the types of assets included in each.

QUESTIONS TO THINK ABOUT

1. Since banks cannot spend the money they create, why should they bother creating it?

2. Banks tend to keep some excess reserves. What factors do you suppose influence the amount they want to keep?

3. What do you think happens to bank reserves before Christmas? After Christmas? What would happen to the money supply at such times if reserves were allowed to fluctuate this way?

4. Why do you think that different banks tend to keep different proportions of their portfolios in primary reserves? In secondary reserves? In loans? In other securities?

5. In our banking system, many banks know that some proportion of the loans they make, when spent, will be redeposited with them. Does this affect the maximum amount of loans that these banks can make at any point in time? Does it affect the likely deposit expansion of the banking system when there are excess reserves?

ANSWERS

Answers to Fill-in Questions

1. assets
   liabilities
   net worth
   balance sheet

2. legal

3. required reserves

4. excess reserves

5. deposit-expansion
   multiplier

6. Liquidity

7. yield to maturity

8. primary

9. secondary

10. municipals

Answers to Problems

1. (a)

Assets		Liabilities	
Legal reserves	−$100	Deposits	−$100

(b)

Assets		Liabilities	
Legal reserves	No change	Deposits	+$500
Loans	+$500		

(c)

Bank A

Assets		Liabilities	
Legal reserves	−$50	Deposits	−$50
Loans	No change		

Bank B

Assets		Liabilities	
Legal reserves	+$50	Deposits	+$50
Loans	No change		

(d)

Bank A

Assets		Liabilities	
Legal reserves	No change	Deposits	−$100
Loans	−$100		

2. (a)

Bank X

Assets		Liabilities	
Legal reserves	+$100	Demand deposits	+$100
Loans	No change	Net worth	No change

(b)

Bank X

Assets		Liabilities	
Legal reserves	$ 5,100	Demand deposits	$50,100
Loans	47,000	Net worth	2,000

(c) $5,010
$90

Bank X

Assets		Liabilities	
Legal reserves	No change	Demand deposits	+$90
Loans	+$90	Net worth	No change

Bank X

Assets		Liabilities	
Legal reserves	$ 5,100	Demand deposits	$50,190
Loans	47,090	Net worth	2,000

(d)

Bank X

Assets		Liabilities	
Legal reserves	−$90	Demand deposits	−$90
Loans	No change	Net worth	No change

Bank Y

Assets		Liabilities	
Legal reserves	+$90	Demand deposits	+$90
Loans	No change	Net worth	No change

Bank X

Assets		Liabilities	
Legal reserves	$ 5,010	Demand deposits	$50,100
Loans	47,090	Net worth	2,000

Bank Y

Assets		Liabilities	
Legal reserves	$ 8,090	Demand deposits	$80,090
Loans	75,000	Net worth	3,000

$5,010
$0
$8,009
$81

(e) $81
increase
$8.10

decrease
$8.10
(f) decrease
$81
$0
increase
$81
increase
$8.10
$72.90
(g) $1,000
(h) $85
$667

3. (a)

Assets		Liabilities	
Legal reserves	−$1,000	Deposits	−$1,000

(b) $800

(c)

Bank A

Assets		Liabilities	
Legal reserves	+$800	Deposits	No change
Securities	− 800		

Bank B

Assets		Liabilities	
Legal reserves	−$800	Deposits	−$800
Securities	No change		

(d) $640
(e) $5,000

Answers to True−False Questions

1.	F	6.	F	10.	F
2.	T	7.	T	11.	?
3.	F	8.	T	12.	T
4.	T	9.	T	13.	F
5.	F				

Answers to Multiple-Choice Questions

1.	c	5.	a	8.	d
2.	c	6.	e	9.	b
3.	a	7.	e	10.	c
4.	e				

CHAPTER 14

Central Banking: Monetary Management and Policy

CHAPTER ORIENTATION

This chapter develops and explains the following concepts:

The quantitative controls of the Federal Reserve: changes in the required reserve ratio, changes in the discount rate, and open-market operations.

The qualitative controls of the Federal Reserve: margin regulations and moral suasion.

The impact of the Treasury on monetary management.

Some strengths and weaknesses of monetary policy.

FILL-IN QUESTIONS

Complete the following sentences. (Answers are given at the end of the chapter.)

1. The interest rate which member banks must pay on their loans from Federal Reserve banks is called the _____ _____.

2. The Federal Reserve's purchases or sales of U.S. government securities in the securities market are called _____ _____.

3. The effective rate of interest on a bond is called the _____.

4. The percentage down payment required when borrowing in order to finance the purchase of stock is called the _____.

5. When the Federal Reserve, orally or in writing, appeals to banks to either expand or restrict credit without compelling their compliance, it is said to be using _____ _____.

PROBLEMS

(Answers are given at the end of the chapter.)

1. In the balance sheet below, Bank A (which is not a monopoly bank) is assumed to be fully loaned up.

Bank A

Vault cash	$ 50	Demand deposits	$1,000
Deposits at the		Net worth	100
Federal Reserve	150		
Loans	900		

(a) The reserve requirement is _____ percent.

(b) Now assume that the Federal Reserve changes the reserve requirement to 10 percent. The legal reserves of Bank A will be $ _____, required reserves will be $ _____, and excess reserves will be $ _____. If Bank A wants to stay fully loaned up, it will (expand/contract) _____ loans by $ _____.

(c) If the banking system as a whole was fully loaned up with reserves of $100,000 before the reserve requirement changed, the change in the reserve requirement will permit the money supply to change by a maximum of $ _____.

2. Assume that the graph shows how much the commercial banking system will borrow per month (net of repayments) from the Federal Reserve at different discount rates. Assume that the banking system is fully loaned up with a reserve requirement of 10 percent and total reserves (borrowed plus unborrowed) of $1,000.

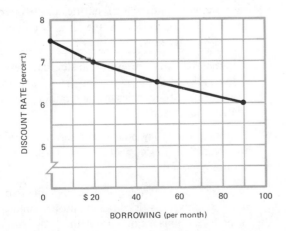

(a) Demand deposits of the banking system are $ _____.

(b) If the discount rate were initially 7.5 percent and the Federal Reserve reduced it to 7.0 percent, banks would (increase/reduce) _____ their borrowing by $ _____ per month. This would permit the money supply to expand by at most $ _____ per month. The same result could have been obtained by open market (sales/purchases) _____ by the Federal Reserve of $ _____ per month.

(c) Assume that the Federal Reserve kept the discount rate at 7.0 percent for 10 months and then raised it back to 7.5 percent. This would permit the same maximum monetary change during this period as would a(n) (increase/decrease) _____ in the reserve requirement at the beginning of the period to _____ percent, assuming that reserves did not change during the period.

3. Assume that the Federal Reserve sells $100 of government securities to a member bank. Assume also that all member banks are fully loaned up with a reserve requirement of 10 percent and that the bank does not pay cash for the security.

(a) Record how this transaction would affect the balance sheets of the bank and of the Federal Reserve.

Federal Reserve Bank	Member Bank

(b) Ultimately, total demand deposits in the banking system will (expand/contract) _____ by $ _____.

(c) If the open-market sale, instead of being to a member bank, had been to an individual who banked with the member bank, reserves of member banks would have (increased/decreased) _____ by $ _____, and the money supply would immediately have (increased/remained the same/decreased)

_____ by $ _____ .

Ultimately, the money supply will have to (increase/

decrease) _____ by a total of

$ _____ .

(d) Putting parts (b) and (c) together, does it matter who

buys the securities which the Federal Reserve is selling?

_____

_____

_____

_____

_____

_____

_____

4. Assume that the banking system is fully loaned up and that, on a particular day, corporations turn over employees' withheld taxes of $100 to the Treasury.

(a) Record this tax transfer in the abbreviated balance sheets below assuming that the Treasury keeps these receipts in a commercial bank.

Federal Reserve Bank	Member Bank

Member-bank reserves have (increased/remained the

same/decreased)

_____ .

(b) Now assume that the Treasury, instead of depositing the tax receipts in a member bank, deposited them in a Federal Reserve bank. Record what would have happened in the abbreviated balance sheets below.

Federal Reserve Bank	Member Bank

Member-bank reserves would have (increased/remained

the same/decreased) _____ .

(c) Looking at parts (a) and (b) together, explain why the

Treasury deposits its tax receipts in commercial banks rather than in Federal Reserve banks. _____

_____

_____

_____

_____

_____

_____

Circle T if the statement is true, F if it is false. (Answers are given at the end of the chapter.)

T F   1. Margin requirements and moral suasion are the qualitative controls of the Federal Reserve.

T F   2. When a commercial bank transfers a portion of its deposits at a Federal Reserve bank to cash in its vault, its legal reserves do not change.

T F   3. The reserve requirements of member banks are graduated according to the size of their demand deposits.

T F   4. If margin requirements are reduced, the deposit-expansion multiplier is increased.

T F   5. An increase in the discount rate reduces member-bank reserves directly, just as open-market sales of securities do.

T F   6. If the Federal Reserve System sells securities in the open market, bank reserves will not fall unless the banks buy these securities themselves.

T F   7. Increasing the discount rate, increasing reserve requirements, and selling securities in the open market all tend to work in the same direction on credit conditions.

T F   8. Commercial banks' reserves will fluctuate less if the Treasury deposits receipts from its sales of government securities in them rather than in the Federal Reserve.

T F   9. By monetary policy not being discriminatory we mean that it affects all sectors of the economy equally.

T F 10. Because monetary policy can be implemented more quickly than fiscal policy, proper timing of policy actions is not a problem.

T F 11. Monetary policy is likely to be more effective to combat inflation than to combat recession because banks must contract the money supply when the Federal Reserve reduces their reserves but need not expand it when the Federal Reserve increases their reserves.

T F 12. A conflict between the Treasury and the Federal Reserve is more likely to exist during an inflation than during a recession.

T F 13. Monetary policy would be more effective than it is if the velocity of money varied more.

SELF-TEST: MULTIPLE-CHOICE QUESTIONS

Circle the letter that corresponds to the best answer. (Answers are given at the end of the chapter.)

1. The main reason that the Federal Reserve requires member banks to hold reserves is:
   (a) To ensure that member banks will be able to meet their liquidity needs.
   (b) For monetary control.
   (c) To provide Reserve banks with cash for their liquidity needs.
   (d) To keep bank profits at a normal level.
   (e) To provide the Treasury with working balances.

2. Which of the following is *not* a monetary policy tool?
   (a) Moral suasion.
   (b) Tax exemption for interest on municipal bonds.
   (c) Changing the discount rate.
   (d) Open-market operations.
   (e) Changing reserve requirements.

3. Assume that the banking system has no excess reserves, a 20 percent legal reserve ratio, and $1,000 in reserves. If the central bank reduced the legal reserve requirement to 10 percent, this would have the same money-expansion potential as:
   (a) Open-market purchases by the central bank of $1,000, assuming that the legal reserve ratio had not been changed.
   (b) Open-market sales by the central bank of $1,000, assuming that the legal reserve ratio had not been changed.
   (c) Open-market purchases by the central bank of $5,000, assuming that the legal reserve ratio had not been changed.
   (d) Open-market sales by the central bank of $5,000, assuming that the legal reserve ratio had not been changed.

(e) Open-market purchases by the central bank of $10,000, assuming that the legal reserve ratio had not been changed.

4. Which of the following would be *least* likely to influence member bank reserves?
   (a) Open-market operations.
   (b) Currency drains from banks during holiday periods.
   (c) Changing the discount rate.
   (d) Banks' withdrawing their deposits from the Federal Reserve and putting the proceeds in their vaults.
   (e) Shifts in deposits from member banks to nonmember banks.

5. Bond prices and bond yields:
   (a) Vary inversely.
   (b) Vary directly.
   (c) Vary inversely or directly, depending on business conditions.
   (d) Are not related.
   (e) Are related in the long run but not in the short run.

6. Monetary policy is less problematical than fiscal policy in the sense that:
   (a) It is easier to forecast for monetary than for fiscal policy.
   (b) Monetary policy is more direct than fiscal policy.
   (c) Monetary policy affects all sectors of the economy equally, whereas fiscal policy does not.
   (d) Monetary policy can be implemented more quickly than fiscal policy.
   (e) Monetary policy is always subject to the approval of Congress, whereas fiscal policy is not.

7. Which of the following is the Federal Reserve *unable* to do?
   (a) Influence member banks.
   (b) Create a climate of monetary ease or restraint.
   (c) Directly determine all interest rates in the economy.
   (d) Influence the degree of fluctuations in the stock market by changing margin requirements.
   (e) Influence the interest rate which the federal government must pay on new bonds.

8. Which of the following would be most expansionary if the reserve requirement were 10 percent and banks were and wanted to stay fully loaned up?
   (a) Federal Reserve purchases of $100 of securities from member banks.
   (b) Federal Reserve sales of government securities of $500.
   (c) A reduction in the discount rate from 4 to 3 ½ percent which caused member banks to borrow $50 more.
   (d) A decrease in the reserve requirement from 10 to 9 percent if total member bank reserves were $10,000.
   (e) There is not enough information to tell.

CHECKPOINT: LEARNING OBJECTIVES

At this point you should be able to do all of the following:

1. Define all of the technical terms and concepts listed at the end of the chapter in the text.

2. Explain how an increase (decrease) in the reserve requirement affects:
   (a) Required reserves.
   (b) Excess reserves.

3. Given a consolidated balance sheet of all member banks and an initial reserve requirement, calculate the amount that banks would have to contract deposits if the reserve requirement were increased to a specified level, and the amount that banks could increase deposits if the reserve requirement were reduced to a specified level.

4. Explain why an increase in the discount rate tends to be contractionary and a decrease in the discount rate tends to be expansionary.

5. Demonstrate, using balance sheets, how open-market sales and purchases of government securities by the Federal Reserve affect member banks, distinguishing between:
   (a) Sales to (purchases from) an individual.
   (b) Sales to (purchases from) a commercial bank.

6. Explain why open-market sales by the Federal Reserve are contractionary and open-market purchases are expansionary.

7. Explain how changes in margin requirements affect activity in the securities market.

8. Describe the use that the Treasury makes of its accounts with commercial banks and with the Federal Reserve.

9. Explain and illustrate with balance sheets why the availability of commercial bank credit will tend to decrease when the Treasury transfers more funds from the commercial banks to the Federal Reserve than it plans to spend, and why the availability of commercial bank credit will tend to increase when the Treasury transfers less funds from commercial banks to the Federal Reserve than it plans to spend.

10. Explain why monetary policy, as compared with fiscal policy, is:
    (a) Nondiscriminatory.
    (b) Flexible.
    (c) Nonpolitical.

11. Describe the problems of monetary policy with regard to:
    (a) Correcting a recession.
    (b) Correcting cost-push and profit-push inflation.

12. Explain why monetary policy may conflict with Treasury objectives.

13. Explain how the existence of financial intermediaries and changes in the velocity of money weaken the effectiveness of monetary policy.

QUESTIONS TO THINK ABOUT

1. Monetary policy is sometimes said to be indirect counter-cyclical policy. In what sense would this be true?

2. It has been argued that it is impossible to draw a precise line between monetary and fiscal policies because fiscal policy has monetary impacts. In what sense is this true?

3. In 1972, the Federal Reserve made check clearing faster, which had the effect of reducing member-bank reserves, and, at the same time, restructured the pattern of reserve requirements, which had the effect of reducing the average reserve requirement. Why did the Fed time these changes to occur at the same time?

4. There are 12 Federal Reserve banks. Would it be possible to conduct 12 different types of monetary policy in the 12 different districts?

5. Nonmember and member banks are subject to different reserve requirements. How would this affect monetary policy, if at all?

6. The Fed conducts open-market operations in U.S government securities. Would it make any difference (with regard to what the Fed was trying to achieve) if instead it conducted these operations by buying and selling pens, dishes, pickles, or any other commodity?

Answers to Fill-in Questions

1. discount rate
2. open-market operations
3. yield to maturity *or* yield
4. margin requirement
5. moral suasion

Answers to Problems

1. (a) 20
   (b) $200
      $100
      $100
      expand
      $100
   (c) $500,000

2. (a) $10,000
   (b) increase
      $20
      $200
      purchases
      $20
   (c) decrease
      8.3 percent (In 10 months, total borrowing would be $200, which would permit the money supply to expand by $2,000. Total demand deposits would thus be $12,000. With $1,000 of legal reserves, in order to have demand deposits of $12,000, the reserve requirement would have to be 8.3 percent: $D = \dfrac{1}{r} R$ or $r = \dfrac{R}{D} = \dfrac{\$1,000}{\$12,000}$.)

3. (a)

Federal Reserve Bank

Government securities	−$100	Member-bank reserve deposits	−$100

Member Bank

Government securities	+$100		
Reserve deposits with Federal Reserve Bank	−$100		

(b) contract
   $1,000

(c) decreased
   $100
   decreased
   $100
   decrease
   $1,000

(d) Although the initial effect on reserves is the same, the initial effect on demand deposits is not. Demand deposits do not change initially if member banks buy the securities, but fall if individuals buy them. Ultimately, however, the total monetary contraction will be the same in both cases.

4. (a)

Federal Reserve Bank

Member Bank

	Corporate demand deposits	−$100
	Treasury deposits	+$100

remained the same

(b)

Federal Reserve Bank

	Member-bank reserve deposits	−$100
	Treasury deposits	+$100

Member Bank

Reserve deposits at Federal Reserve banks	−$100	Corporate demand deposits	−$100

decreased

(c) If the Treasury deposited tax receipts in Federal Reserve banks, every time corporations transferred withheld taxes to the Treasury, member-bank reserves would decline. This would create problems for monetary control.

Answers to True–False Questions

1. T	6. F	10. F
2. T	7. T	11. T
3. T	8. T	12. T
4. F	9. F	13. F
5. F		

Answers to Multiple-Choice Questions

1. b	5. a
2. b	6. d
3. a	7. c
4. d	8. d

CHAPTER 15

Synthesis: Macroeconomic Equilibrium

CHAPTER ORIENTATION

This chapter develops and explains the following concepts:

The quantity theory of money, which concludes that a change in the money supply results in an equiproportionate change in the price level.

Determination of the market and real rates of interest in classical theory.

The liquidity-preference theory of interest rates, which states that the interest rate is determined by the demand for and supply of money.

The determinants of liquidity preference.

A simplified model of income determination and macro-economic equilibrium.

FILL-IN QUESTIONS

Complete the following sentences. (Answers are given at the end of the chapter.)

1. The average number of times per year that a dollar is spent on purchasing the economy's annual flow of final goods and services is called the _____ _____ of money.

2. The _____ _____ states that the level of prices in the economy is directly proportional to the quantity of money in circulation, such that a given percentage change in the stock of money will cause an equal percentage change in the price level in the same direction.

3. The anticipated rate of return over cost on an additional unit of investment is called the _____ _____ _____.

4. The price paid for the use of loanable funds over a period is called _____. The actual money rate that prevails is called the _____ rate. The rate

measured in terms of goods is called the _____ rate.

5. The body of economic thought that originated with J. M. Keynes in the 1930s is called _____.

6. The _____ motive for holding money expresses the idea that people want to hold a portion of their assets in the form of money in order to engage in regular daily spending activities. The _____ motive expresses the idea that people want to hold a portion of their assets in the form of money to meet possible unforeseen conditions. And the _____ motive expresses the idea that people want to hold a portion of their assets in the form of money to take advantage of a change in interest rates.

7. The _____ _____ _____ states that the interest rate is determined by the demand for and supply of money.

8. The horizontal segment of the liquidity-preference curve is called the _____.

PROBLEM

(Answers are given at the end of the chapter.)

1. Answer the following questions by referring to the diagram on page 129. Assume for the moment that $L = L_1$, $MEI = MEI_1$, $C = C_1$, and that there is no government. Also, assume that when income changes, L does not shift.

   (a) The equilibrium interest rate is _____ percent, the equilibrium level of investment is $ _____, and the equilibrium level of income is $ _____.

   (b) Now assume that the full-employment level of income is $700, and that the Federal Reserve System decides to increase the money supply in order to bring the economy to this level. For income to equal $700,

investment must equal $ _____, which requires an interest rate of _____ percent. Hence, the money supply must rise to $ _____.

   (c) Now assume that $L = L_2$, $MEI = MEI_1$, and $C = C_1$. To reach income of $700, investment must rise to $ _____, which requires an interest rate of _____ percent. This requires a money supply of $ _____. Thus, the (flatter/steeper) _____ the liquidity-preference curve, the more the money supply must increase in order to get a given increase in income.

   (d) Now assume that $L = L_1$, $MEI = MEI_2$, and $C = C_1$. To reach income of $700, investment must rise to $ _____, which requires an interest rate of _____ percent. This requires a money supply of about $ _____. Hence, the (flatter/steeper) _____ _____ the MEI, the more the money supply must increase in order to get a given increase in income.

   (e) Now assume that $L = L_1$, $MEI = MEI_1$, and $C = C_2$. Note that equilibrium income is $ _____ but that the MPC corresponding to C_2 is greater than the MPC corresponding to C_1. To reach income of $700, investment must rise to $ _____, which requires an interest rate of _____ percent. This requires a money supply of about $ _____. Hence, the (greater/smaller) _____ the MPC, the more the money supply must increase in order to get a given increase in income.

   (f) Putting all of this together, in order to get a given increase in income, the money supply must increase more: the (flatter/steeper) _____ is L; the (flatter/steeper) _____ is the MEI; the (greater/smaller) _____ is the MPC.

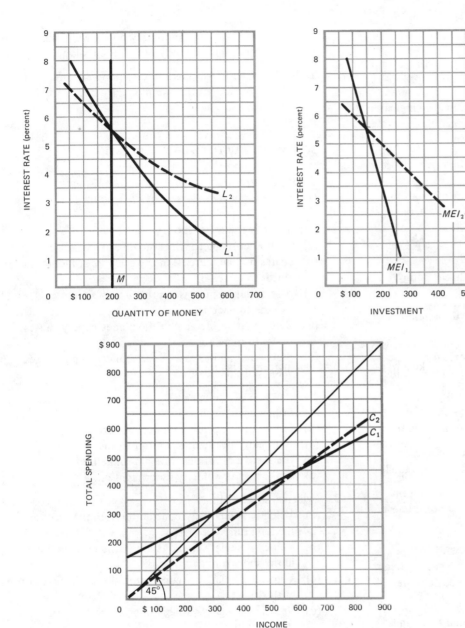

(g) Finally, recognize that as the money supply rises and income rises, the demand for money does, in fact, increase. Explain carefully how this affects the equilibrium level of income when the money supply increases by a given amount. _____

_____

_____

_____

_____

_____

_____

_____

_____

_____

_____

Circle T if the statement is true, F if it is false. (Answers are given at the end of the chapter.)

T F 1. The equation of exchange says that an increase in the money supply leads to an equiproportionate increase in the price level.

T F 2. If the money supply is $100, the price level is $2, and the quantity of final output sold during a year is 150, the number of times that each dollar is spent in purchasing the economy's final output during the year is 3.

T F 3. $MV = PQ$ is always true.

T F 4. Classical economists believed that V and Q tended to be constant.

T F 5. In the long run, V does appear to be relatively constant.

T F 6. The quantity theory is very useful for predicting short-run changes in the price level on the basis of changes in M.

T F 7. Modern quantity theorists argue that V is constant in the short run but not in the long run.

T F 8. Classical economists argued that people who save always invest their saving in capital goods.

T F 9. If the market rate of interest were 4 percent and prices were rising, the real rate of interest would be less than 4 percent.

T F 10. The transactions demand for money exists because people have to bridge the gap between the time income is received and outlays are made.

T F 11. The transactions and precautionary demands for money depend primarily on the rate of interest.

T F 12. When interest rates are low and people expect them to rise, they expect bond prices to rise as well.

T F 13. The quantity of money demanded depends positively (directly) on income and inversely on the interest rate.

T F 14. If the money supply is constant and income rises, we would expect the interest rate to rise.

T F 15. If investment is unresponsive to changes in the interest rate, monetary policy will be unable to pull the economy out of a recession.

T F 16. The flatter the liquidity-preference function, the more effective monetary policy will be.

SELF-TEST: MULTIPLE-CHOICE QUESTIONS

Circle the letter that corresponds to the best answer. (Answers are given at the end of the chapter.)

1. The quantity theory of money:
   (a) Is another name for the equation of exchange.
   (b) States that an increase in the velocity of money causes prices to increase.
   (c) States that an increase in the money supply causes real income to decrease.
   (d) States that an increase in the money supply causes prices to increase.
   (e) States that an increase in the money supply causes velocity to decrease.

2. The equation of exchange:
   (a) Is an identity.
   (b) Is a theory of price-level determination.
   (c) Is a theory of income determination.
   (d) Is a theory of interest-rate determination.
   (e) Is a theory of velocity determination.

3. Evidence suggests that:
   (a) Velocity is relatively constant in both the short and the long run.
   (b) Velocity is relatively constant in the long run but not in the short run.
   (c) Velocity is relatively constant in the short run but not in the long run.
   (d) Velocity is highly variable in both the short run and the long run.
   (e) Velocity cannot be measured in either the short run or the long run.

4. Modern quantity theorists argue that:
   (a) Velocity is highly variable.
   (b) Velocity is perfectly constant.
   (c) Velocity varies but its variation is predictable.
   (d) Velocity is unimportant.
   (e) Changes in velocity are the primary determinant of changes in GNP.

5. Classical economists argued that:
   (a) Interest rates fall when saving increases, other things remaining the same.

(b) Interest rates fall when investment increases, other things remaining the same.

(c) Interest rates are determined by the supply of and demand for money.

(d) Real interest rates fall whenever prices fall.

(e) Interest rates rise whenever income rises.

6. Classical economists argued that:

(a) Savers are investors.

(b) Investors are savers.

(c) Saving will equal investment only at high levels of income.

(d) When saving is greater than investment, the interest rate will rise.

(e) Saving will tend to equal investment as long as the interest rate if flexible.

7. If the market rate of interest is 6 percent and prices are rising by 2 percent per year, the real rate of interest equals:

(a) 8 percent.

(b) 6 percent.

(c) 4 percent.

(d) 3 percent.

(e) 2 percent.

8. Modern quantity theorists argue that increases in the money supply:

(a) Cause prices to rise and market interest rates to fall.

(b) Cause both prices and market interest rates to rise.

(c) Do not affect prices but cause market interest rates to rise.

(d) Do not affect market interest rates but cause prices to rise.

(e) Do not affect either prices or market interest rates.

9. According to Keynesian theory, a decrease in income will:

(a) Decrease the speculative demand for money.

(b) Decrease the speculative and precautionary demands for money.

(c) Decrease the speculative and transactions demands for money.

(d) Decrease the precautionary and transactions demands for money.

(e) Decrease the speculative, precautionary, and transactions demands for money.

10. If the quantity of money demanded exceeds the quantity of money supplied:

(a) The interest rate will fall.

(b) The interest rate will fall, causing liquidity preference to fall.

(c) The interest rate will rise.

(d) The interest rate will rise, causing liquidity preference to rise.

(e) The interest rate will not change, but liquidity preference will fall until equilibrium is reached.

11. According to Keynesian theory, if the money supply increases:

(a) The transactions demand for money decreases.

(b) Liquidity preference decreases.

(c) Interest rates rise.

(d) Interest rates fall.

(e) Interest rates fall, and the *MEI* shifts to the right.

12. If the *MEI* increases (i.e., the curve shifts to the right), we would expect:

(a) Income and the interest rate to rise.

(b) Income and the interest rate to fall.

(c) Income to rise and the interest rate to fall.

(d) Income to fall and the interest rate to rise.

(e) Income to fall but the interest rate to remain unchanged.

13. A reduction in the money supply will have a greater effect on real GNP:

(a) The steeper the *MEI* curve.

(b) The flatter the *LP* curve.

(c) The greater the *MPC*.

(d) The more that prices fall as *M* decreases.

(e) The smaller the multiplier.

14. An increase in the money supply will have no effect on the economy if:

(a) The *MPC* is very small.

(b) The *MEI* is flat.

(c) The economy is in a liquidity trap.

(d) All of the above.

(e) None of the above.

CHECKPOINT: LEARNING OBJECTIVES

At this point you should be able to do all of the following:

1. Define all of the technical terms and concepts listed at the end of the chapter in the text.

2. State the equation of exchange, and explain what it says.

3. State the assumptions about velocity and output which underlie the quantity theory of money, and describe what the evidence suggests about the validity of the velocity assumptions.

4. Describe what modern quantity theorists believe about velocity, and the policy implications of their beliefs.

5. Explain the classical theory of the determination of the market rate of interest.

6. Describe the relationship between the market rate of interest and the real rate of interest, and explain why modern quantity theorists believe that the money supply affects the market rate as well as the price level.

7. Explain how Keynes's theory of interest-rate determination differed from the classical economists' theory, and what Keynes thought the interest rate was payment for.

8. Distinguish among the following motives for holding money. Discuss the determinants of each.
   (a) The transactions motive.
   (b) The precautionary motive.
   (c) The speculative motive.

9. Explain what happens to the equilibrium interest rate if:
   (a) National income rises.
   (b) The money supply increases.

10. Explain why the effectiveness of monetary policy depends on:
    (a) The shape of the liquidity-preference curve.
    (b) The shape of the *MEI* curve.
    (c) The size of the multiplier.

11. Explain how the existence of a liquidity trap would influence the effectiveness of monetary policy.

12. Summarize the theory of income determination, and state the conditions for macroeconomic equilibrium.

QUESTIONS TO THINK ABOUT

1. Many economists today reject the quantity theory of money. Why?

2. During parts of the latter 1960s interest rates were very high by historical standards. Yet some economists argued that they were really not high at all. Can you explain this apparent paradox?

3. Some economists argue that the money supply should be increased at a constant rate over time — a rate equal to the rate of growth of full-employment real GNP. They say that this would give easy money in recessions and tight money in inflations. Do you agree?

4. "Only if investment is quite sensitive to changes in the rate of interest will monetary policy be a successful stabilization tool." Do you agree?

5. Does the theory of interest-rate determination have any implications for the multiplier analysis you learned previously?

6. In boom periods we typically see both interest rates and the rate of investment rising. Does this imply that investment depends directly (as opposed to inversely) on the rate of interest?

7. During the Great Depression, monetary policy appeared to be unable to provide much stimulus to the economy. Based on the theory you have learned so far, how would you explain its failure?

ANSWERS

Answers to Fill-in Questions

1. income velocity
2. quantity theory of money
3. marginal efficiency of
   investment
4. interest
   market
   real
5. the New Economics
6. transactions
   precautionary
   speculative
7. liquidity-preference theory
   of interest
8. liquidity trap

Answers to Problem

1. (a) 5 ½
       $150
       $600
   (b) $200
       3 ½
       $350
   (c) $200
       3 ½
       $500
       flatter
   (d) $200
       5
       $240
       steeper
   (e) $600
       $175
       4 ½
       $275
       smaller
   (f) flatter
       steeper
       smaller
   (g) When the money supply increases, the interest rate will
       start to fall, investment will start to rise, and income
       will start to rise. But the rise in income increases the
       demand for money, which will keep the interest rate
       from falling as much as it would have had the demand
       for money not increased. Hence, investment will not
       rise as much, and the new equilibrium level of income
       will not be as high as it would have been, had the
       demand for money not increased.

Answers to True–False Questions

1.	F	9.	T
2.	T	10.	T
3.	T	11.	F
4.	T	12.	F
5.	T	13.	T
6.	F	14.	T
7.	F	15.	T
8.	F	16.	F

Answers to Multiple-Choice Questions

1. d
2. a
3. b
4. c
5. a
6. e
7. c
8. b
9. d (Note that the
   speculative demand is
   assumed to depend
   only on the interest
   rate.)
10. c
11. d
12. a (Note that the increase
    in the *MEI* causes in-
    vestment and therefore
    income to rise, and the
    increase in income in-
    creases the demand for
    money.)
13. c
14. c

CHAPTER 16

Efficiency, Stability, and Growth: Approaches to Public Policy

CHAPTER ORIENTATION

This chapter develops and explains the following concepts:

The disagreement between the fiscalists and monetarists on the need for and usefulness of discretionary stabilization policies.

The money-supply rule, and the general agreement among fiscalists and monetarists regarding the importance of a more steady rate of monetary expansion.

The conflict between full employment and price stability as indicated by the Phillips curve, and some reasons for this conflict.

Some factors that influence the position of the Phillips curve.

Okun's Law, and the degree to which economic growth results in a reduction in unemployment.

Some arguments for and against wage–price controls and economic planning.

FILL-IN QUESTIONS

Complete the following sentences. (Answers are given at the end of the chapter.)

1. A graphic representation of the relationship between the rate of inflation and the rate of unemployment is called

   _____.

2. _____ states that unemployment decreases (increases) less than 1 percent for each percentage point that the annual growth of real GNP exceeds (falls short of) its long-term average.

3. The _____ is a body of economic thought which emerged in the 1930s from the ideas of John Maynard Keynes.

4. The idea that the Federal Reserve should expand the nation's money supply at the economy's growth rate or capacity to produce is called the _____

   _____.

5. A detailed method, formulated beforehand, for achieving specific economic objectives by governing the activities and interrelationships of those economic organisms that have an influence on the desired outcome is called a(n)_____

   _____.

Circle T if the statement is true, F if it is false. (Answers are given at the end of the chapter.)

T F 1. Fiscalists believe that the economy is inherently stable and would tend to achieve full employment if left alone.

T F 2. Monetarists believe that fiscal policy should be used only when the economy is in a serious inflation or recession.

T F 3. Monetarists believe that changes in the money supply induce changes in economic activity because they produce changes in spending.

T F 4. Fiscalists and monetarists tend to agree that changes in the money supply do exert an important influence on economic activity.

T F 5. The Phillips curve tells us that the lower the rate of unemployment, the higher the price level.

T F 6. The greater the rate of inflation, the more the Phillips curve shifts to the right.

T F 7. Extension of antitrust laws would tend to lower The Phillips curve, whereas fiscal policies aimed at reducing structural unemployment would tend to raise it.

T F 8. Restrictive monetary and fiscal policies will tend to push an economy to the right along a given Phillips curve, other things being equal.

T F 9. If the natural unemployment rate is 7 percent, there is no possible way ever to reduce unemployment below this without serious inflationary consequences.

T F 10. Increasing both reserve requirements and personal income taxes would be an appropriate policy mix aimed at promoting economic growth without inflation, other things remaining the same.

T F 11. If the U.S. economy were to grow at 6 percent next year, then, according to Okun's Law, the unemployment rate should decline by at least 2 percent.

T F 12. Government, through minimum wage laws and other price-support policies, contributes to the inflationary bias in the economy.

T F 13. Economic planning and wage–price controls may produce greater social costs than inflation itself.

Circle the letter that corresponds to the best answer. (Answers are given at the end of the chapter.)

1. According to the fiscalists:
    (a) Monetary policy is useless as a tool of economic stabilization.
    (b) Fiscal policy is useless as a tool of economic stabilization.
    (c) Both monetary and fiscal policies are useless as tools of economic stabilization.
    (d) Both monetary and fiscal policies are useful as tools of economic stabilization and their use should be coordinated to achieve desired goals.
    (e) Both monetary and fiscal policies are useful as tools of economic stabilization, but because they tend to offset each other, only one should be used at a time.

2. Monetarists believe that:
    (a) Fiscal policy is useful for economic stabilization.
    (b) The money supply should remain constant over time.
    (c) Business cycles in the past have resulted primarily from changes in the rate of growth of the money supply.
    (d) The economy is inherently unstable.
    (e) Government spending exerts an overwhelmingly important influence on business activity.

3. Adherence to the money supply rule over time would result in:
    (a) A constant money supply.
    (b) A money supply whose rate of growth varies with the stage of the business cycle.
    (c) A declining rate of interest.
    (d) Accelerating inflation whenever real economic growth exceeds its long-run trend.
    (e) A constant rate of growth of the money supply equal to the economy's growth in productive capacity.

4. If prices rise before full employment is reached and policy-makers want to stop inflation but attain full employment:
    (a) A restrictive monetary policy should be applied.
    (b) A restrictive fiscal policy should be applied.
    (c) A restrictive monetary and a restrictive fiscal policy should be applied.

(d) A restrictive monetary but an easy fiscal policy should be applied.

(e) Use of monetary and fiscal policies alone cannot assure both full employment and price stability.

5. Which of the following is *not* a reason that the goals of full employment and price stability appear to conflict with each other?

(a) High employment increases the aggressiveness with which unions push for wage increases.

(b) High profits and a good business outlook encourage firms to pass on higher costs in the form of higher prices.

(c) Labor shortages tend to push up wages even in areas that are nonunionized.

(d) Resources become increasingly scarce and their prices rise as full employment is approached.

(e) Monetary and fiscal policies applied to cool down the economy tend to be in conflict with each other.

6. A Phillips curve shows:

(a) The relationship between wages and prices in an economy.

(b) The relationship between wages and unemployment in an economy.

(c) The relationship between prices and unemployment in an economy.

(d) The relationship between the rate of change in prices and the rate of unemployment in an economy.

(e) The relationship between the rate of change in prices and the rate of change in unemployment in an economy.

7. If a Phillips curve for an economy has an L shape:

(a) Monetary and fiscal policies can never reduce unemployment.

(b) Worsening inflation is inevitable.

(c) It is impossible ever to achieve a situation where only frictional and structural unemployment exist.

(d) No trade-off between unemployment and inflation is possible.

(e) It is necessary to improve labor markets if unemployment is to be reduced below the natural rate.

8. Which of the following would *not* shift the Phillips curve for an economy?

(a) A change in the rate of inflation.

(b) A change in the degree of competition among business firms.

(c) A change in the degree of competition in resource markets.

(d) A change in the proportion of the labor force which is unskilled.

(e) An increase in the degree to which the government fixes prices.

9. Which of the following is true of wage–price controls?

(a) They rigidify the price system and cause resource misallocation.

(b) They may reduce workers' incentives.

(c) They tend to institutionalize inflation.

(d) Their administration wastes manpower.

(e) All of the above.

10. Those who favor wage–price controls argue that:

(a) There is no competition left in the U.S. economy.

(b) Inflation has become so institutionalized that only controls can contain it.

(c) The competitive market philosophy is a myth based on faulty logic.

(d) Competitive markets are more wasteful of resources than are markets governed by wage–price controls.

(e) Wage–price controls assure efficient allocation of resources.

11. Those who oppose economic planning argue that:

(a) Planning would create a new federal bureaucracy.

(b) The free market would, with planning, be replaced by governmental authority and coercion.

(c) Corporations would tend to dominate the planning office.

(d) Government is no more adept at planning than is business.

(e) All of the above.

CHECKPOINT: LEARNING OBJECTIVES

At this point you should be able to do all of the following:

1. Define all of the technical terms and concepts listed at the end of the chapter in the text.

2. Explain why fiscalists believe that government stabilization policies should be used, and describe what these policies are.

3. Explain the monetarists' belief that the money supply influences the level of economic activity, and the logic behind the "money-supply rule."

4. Explain the way in which fiscalists and monetarists are in fundamental agreement with regard to monetary policy.

5. Give several reasons why the general level of prices begins to rise before full employment is reached.

6. Explain what an L-shaped Phillips curve means and describe the type of policy needed to reduce the natural unemployment rate.

7. Explain how each of the following influences the height of the Phillips curve:
   (a) Downward wage and price rigidity.
   (b) The proportion of the labor force consisting of unskilled and inexperienced workers.
   (c) Government price-fixing policies.

8. Explain some types of policies that would tend to lower the Phillips curve in the long run.

9. Describe the fiscal–monetary policy mix that would help an economy promote economic growth without inflation.

10. State what Okun's Law implies about the possibility of reducing unemployment through economic growth.

11. Explain how wage–price controls lead to:
    (a) The misallocation of resources.
    (b) A decrease in productivity.
    (c) The institutionalization of inflation.

12. Explain why some economists favor some wage–price controls despite these problems.

13. Explain why many people oppose economic planning.

QUESTIONS TO THINK ABOUT

1. Precisely what kinds of policies would be useful in reducing the natural unemployment rate? Have any such policies ever been tried in the United States? Would they interfere with the market mechanism?

2. Assume that the economy is in a recession and you are asked what economic policy should be pursued. How would you answer if you were a fiscalist? If you were a monetarist?

3. "A Phillips curve can tell us about the past but it is not a useful tool for establishing policy guidelines for the future." Do you agree?

4. "Wage–price controls are good stopgap measures to cool down an overheated economy but are not useful or effective under most circumstances." Do you agree?

5. On the basis of the current state of the economy and the changes it has undergone in the last several years, would you say that efforts toward economic stabilization have been successful? If not, can you explain why?

6. Would planning be consistent with democracy? With free markets?

ANSWERS

Answers to Fill-in Questions

1. a Phillips curve
2. Okun's Law
3. New Economics
4. money-supply rule
5. economic plan

Answers to True–False Questions

1. F

2. F (They do not think that fiscal policy should ever be used for stabilization.)

3. T

4. T

5. F (The Phillips curve shows the relationship between the rate of unemployment and the rate of change of prices — not the price level.)

6. F

7. F

8. T

9. F

10. F

11. F

12. T

13. T

Answers to Multiple-Choice Questions

1. d
2. c
3. e
4. e
5. e
6. d
7. e
8. a
9. e
10. b
11. e

PART 4

Economic Growth and Resource Policies

CHAPTER 17

Understanding Economic Growth

CHAPTER ORIENTATION

This chapter develops and explains the following concepts:

The classical theory of economic growth, in which wages and profit per unit of capital tend toward a long-run level of subsistence, while rents increase.

The factors that determine a country's rate of growth.

The degree to which these different factors have, in fact, been responsible for growth in the United States.

A modern theory of growth, in which it is shown that if aggregate demand is to equal growing full-employment productive potential over time, the rate of investment must continually increase.

FILL-IN QUESTIONS

Complete the following sentences. (Answers are given at the end of the chapter.)

1. _____ is the rate of increase in an economy's real output or income over time. It can be measured either as (1) the rise in _____ over time, or (2) the rise in _____ over time.

2. The idea that wages will tend toward a level determined by biological and customary needs is called the _____.

3. The idea that population tends to increase geometrically and the means of subsistence tend to increase, at most, arithmetically is called the _____.

4. An increase in the stock of capital relative to other factors of production is called _____.

5. The idea that producers must set aside part of their capital out of which to pay wages is called the _____ _____ theory.

6. The relationship between the economy's stock of real capital and its output or productive capacity is called the

_____.

PROBLEMS

(Answers are given at the end of the chapter.)

1. Answer the following questions by referring to the diagram of the classical model of economic growth.

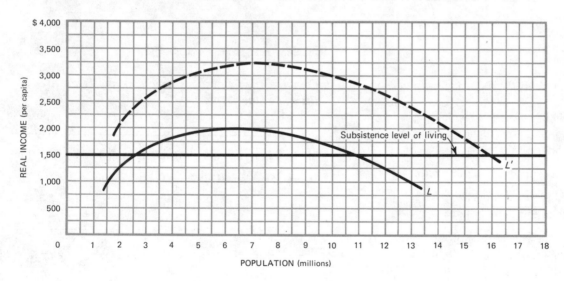

(a) If the average product of labor is L, the optimum population is _____ because at this population

_____

_____.

(b) According to the Malthusian theory, if society had this population, the wage would be (above/at/below) _____ the subsistence level and the birth rate would _____ until population reached about

_____. If population rose above this, the wage would be (above/at/

below) _____ the subsistence level and the birth rate would _____ until population became about

_____.

(c) If for some reason labor productivity increased and the average product of labor curve shifted to L', the optimum population would be _____, but the actual population would tend to be _____ _____. Hence, an increase in labor productivity alone (will/will not) _____ improve the standard of living.

2. Assume that the capital–output ratio is 2:1, the economy is at full-employment equilibrium with NNP = $16 million, and that there is no government or foreign trade.

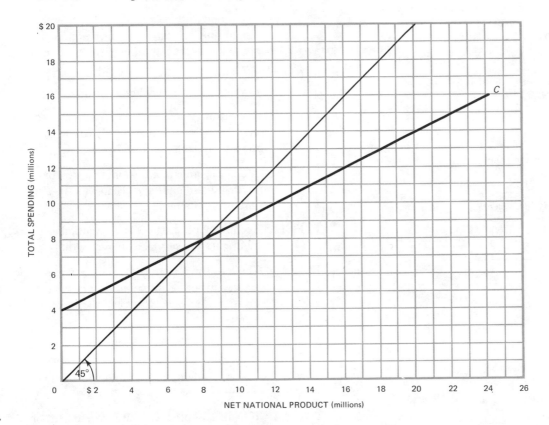

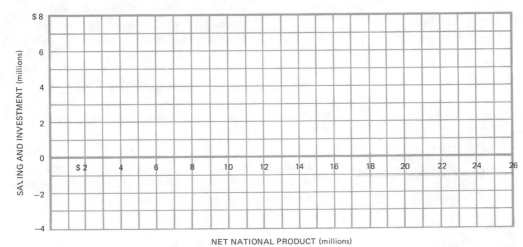

(a) In the lower graph, draw the saving function.

(b) In this year, investment must be $ _____ million. Draw this in the same graph and label it I_1.

(c) In the next year, full-employment output will be

$ _____ million, and investment must be $ _____ million in order to maintain full employment. Draw this in the same graph and label it I_2.

(d) In the third year, full-employment output will be

$ _____ million, and investment must be

$ _____ million in order to maintain full employment. Draw this in the same graph and label it I_3.

(e) Thus, we see that if the economy is to remain at full employment over time, investment must _____

_____ .

3. (a) Given that the APS equals 0.2, that the capital–output ratio is 4:1, and that there is no government or foreign trade, complete the following table:

Year	Full-employment NNP	Saving (= investment)	Resulting increase in output
1	$100	$_____	$_____
2	_____	_____	_____
3	_____	_____	_____
4	_____	_____	_____

(b) The full-employment growth rate is _____ percent per year.

SELF-TEST: TRUE–FALSE QUESTIONS

Circle T if the statement is true, F if it is false. (Answers are given at the end of the chapter.)

T F 1. If during a year GNP rises by $1,000, we know that economic growth has occurred.

T F 2. According to the classical theory, economic growth does not make workers richer on a per capita basis.

T F 3. In classical growth theory, population tends toward its optimal level.

T F 4. According to the wages-fund theory, the real wage of labor depends directly on the size of the capital stock relative to the number of workers in the economy.

T F 5. The easiest way to improve the standard of living in the long run, according to classical theory, would be to discover new resources or develop new productive techniques every once in a while.

T F 6. One way a country could break out of a "Malthusian trap" would be for its people, through population control and other measures, to strive for a standard of living which is higher than minimal subsistence.

T F 7. According to the classical view of growth, diminishing returns will ultimately lead to a reduction in the rate of profit, wages, and rent.

T F 8. Historical evidence supports the classical theory of the returns to the factors of production.

T F 9. The quantity and quality of a nation's economic resources are not necessarily fixed, even if the nation has a fixed land area.

T F 10. A country undergoing economic growth normally also undergoes changes in its structure of production.

T F 11. Technological progress and invention are, for all intents and purposes, the same thing.

T F 12. The most important sources of increases in per capita output in this country have been increases in the labor force and the stock of capital.

T F 13. Other things being equal, the more an economy grows, the higher is the level of investment needed to maintain full employment at capacity output.

T F 14. If in an economy without a government or foreign trade the APC equals 0.8 and the capital–output ratio equals 6:1, the full employment growth rate equals 13.3 percent.

SELF-TEST: MULTIPLE-CHOICE QUESTIONS

Circle the letter that corresponds to the best answer. (Answers are given at the end of the chapter.)

1. If during a year GNP increases by 5 percent, prices increase by 2 percent and population remains the same, the economy is growing at about:
   (a) 7 percent.
   (b) 6 percent.
   (c) 5 percent.
   (d) 4 percent.
   (e) 3 percent.

2. According to the classical theory of economic growth:
   (a) The returns to labor, capital, and land must ultimately increase.

(b) The returns to labor and capital must ultimately increase, and the returns to land must ultimately decrease.

(c) The returns to labor must ultimately decrease, and the returns to capital and land must ultimately increase.

(d) The returns to labor and capital must ultimately decrease, and the returns to land must ultimately increase.

(e) The returns to labor, capital, and land must ultimately decrease.

3. Which of the following would tend to help an economy pull itself out of a "Malthusian trap"?
   (a) Continuous increases in labor productivity.
   (b) Movement of a substantial proportion of the population to underpopulated areas.
   (c) Cultural changes which lead to an increase in the minimally acceptable standard of living.
   (d) All of the above.
   (e) None of the above.

4. According to the classical theory, the reason that the returns to land, labor, and capital behave as they do in the growth process is that:
   (a) All factors will experience diminishing returns over time.
   (b) Capital and labor will experience diminishing returns as land becomes increasingly scarce.
   (c) Capitalists exploit or appropriate part of the output that belongs to labor.
   (d) Increased labor productivity makes workers more aggressive in their wage demands.
   (e) The capital stock remains constant over time as the supply of labor increases.

5. Historical evidence suggests that:
   (a) Factors never experience diminishing returns.
   (b) Labor productivity has increased sufficiently over time to offset the tendency toward diminishing returns.
   (c) The returns to land, labor, and capital have behaved in the way that the classical model suggests.
   (d) The returns to labor have declined rather markedly, but the returns to capital and land have not.
   (e) The returns to capital have increased rather markedly at the expense of the returns to labor.

6. Which of the following is *not* a factor that influences the rate of economic growth (assuming that demand is sufficient to maintain full employment)?
   (a) The quantity and quality of human resources.
   (b) The quantity and quality of natural resources.
   (c) The propensity to save.

(d) The rate of technological progress.
(e) They all influence the rate of economic growth.

7. For substantial economic growth to occur:
   (a) Population must remain constant.
   (b) People must be willing to spend their incomes on consumption goods.
   (c) The government must tax away excess profits.
   (d) The political, social, and cultural environment, as well as the economic environment, must be conducive.
   (e) The capital–output ratio must be high.

8. According to studies of U.S. economic growth, the single most important source of our increase in total output has been:
   (a) Increases in the labor force.
   (b) Increases in the stock of capital.
   (c) "Technical progress."
   (d) Discovery of new raw materials.
   (e) A continuously increasing savings rate.

9. If the *APS* equals 0.3, the full-employment growth rate is 5 percent, and there is no government or foreign trade, the capital–output ratio must be:
   (a) 1.5:1
   (b) 2.7:1
   (c) 6:1
   (d) 8:1
   (e) 1.4:1

10. For a growing economy to sustain sufficient demand to utilize fully its growing productive capacity, net investment must:
    (a) Increase over time.
    (b) Remain constant over time.
    (c) Decrease over time.
    (d) Increase in the early stages of growth and decrease in the later stages.
    (e) Decrease in the early stages of growth and increase in the later stages.

CHECKPOINT: LEARNING OBJECTIVES

At this point you should be able to do all of the following:

1. Define all of the technical terms and concepts listed at the end of the chapter in the text.

2. State the assumptions underlying the classical theory of economic growth with regard to:
   (a) The changes in the average product of labor which take place as population increases.
   (b) The determinants of population growth.

3. Explain why the classical theory of economic growth concludes that wages will tend toward the subsistence level.

4. State the ways in which Malthus thought that a society could prevent subsistence living.

5. Discuss how, theoretically, each of the following could help a country escape from a "Malthusian trap":
   (a) Shifting the population geographically.
   (b) Developing new resources and production techniques.
   (c) Raising the "subsistence level" to an aspiration level.

6. Explain why classical growth theory implies:
   (a) A subsistence level of profits.
   (b) Rising rents.

7. Explain the wages-fund theory, and state what the size of the wages fund and the level of wages depend on.

8. Describe and explain the U.S. long-run trends in:
   (a) Real wages.
   (b) Interest rates.
   (c) Rents.

9. Explain how each of the following influences the rate of growth in an economy:
   (a) The quantity and quality of human resources.
   (b) The quantity and quality of "natural" resources.
   (c) The accumulation of capital.
   (d) Specialization and the scale of production.
   (e) The rate of technological progress.
   (f) Environmental factors.

10. If the determinants of growth are considered to be growth of the labor force, growth of capital, and "technical progress," explain:

(a) What is meant by "technical progress."
(b) How important "technical progress" has been in the growth of the United States.

11. Explain and show graphically why, in the absence of government and international sectors, increasing levels of investment are necessary to sustain full employment when there is growing productive capacity.

12. Explain and demonstrate why the full-employment growth rate is equal to the average propensity to save divided by the capital–output ratio.

QUESTIONS TO THINK ABOUT

1. "If the subsistence level of income is defined as a culturally acceptable level, there is nothing dismal about the conclusions of classical growth theory." Do you agree?

2. Studies have been done which conclude that more of our growth has been attributable to technological change than to capital formation. But is it really possible to separate the two since new capital embodies new technology?

3. Does it really make sense to argue that a country's supply of natural resources is not fixed? If so, why?

4. Thinking back on the development of our country, cite several ways in which economic growth was accompanied by changes in the structure of society.

5. "A decrease in the capital–output ratio increases society's productive potential but makes growth more difficult." Do you agree?

Answers to Fill-in Questions

1. Economic growth
   total real GNP *or* NNP
   per capita real GNP *or* NNP

2. subsistence theory of wages
   (*or* the iron *or* brazen law
   of wages)

3. Malthusian theory of
   population

4. capital deepening

5. wages-fund

6. capital–output ratio

Answers to Problems

1. (a) 6.5 million
       average output per
       person is maximized
   (b) above
       increase
       10.75 million

   below
   decrease
   10.75 million
   (c) 7 million
       16 million
       will not

2. (a), (b), (c), (d)

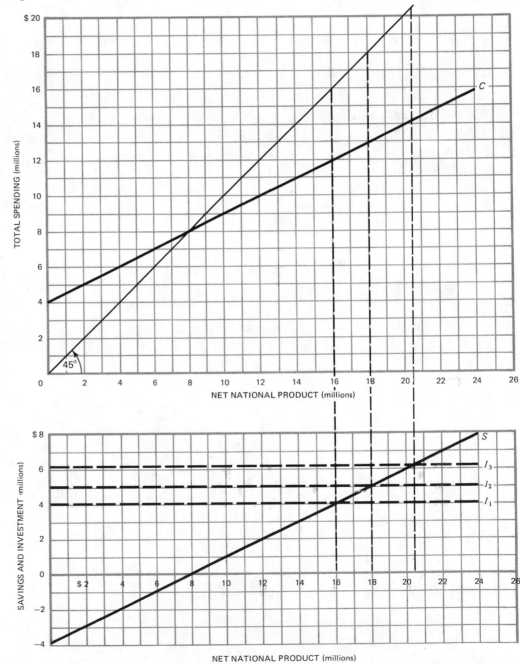

(b) $4
(c) $18
$5
(d) $20.5
$6.25
(e) continuously increase

3. (a)

Full-employment NNP	Saving (= investment)	Resulting increase in output
$100	$20	$5
105	21	5.25
110.25	22.05	5.51
115.76	23.15	

(b) 5 percent

Answers to True–False Questions

1. F (Prices may have risen enough to cause *real* GNP to fall, or population may have grown enough to make real GNP per capita fall.)

2. T   9. T
3. F   10. T
4. T   11. F
5. F   12. F
6. T   13. T
7. F   14. F
8. F

Answers to Multiple-Choice Questions

1. e   6. e
2. d   7. d
3. d   8. c
4. b   9. c
5. b   10. a

CHAPTER 18

Problems of Economic Growth

CHAPTER ORIENTATION

This chapter develops and explains the following concepts:

Some major trends in the economy since 1900, and a comparison between growth in the United States and other developed economies.

The sources of growth in the U.S. economy since the turn of the century.

How to determine the rate of growth of an economy, and how long it would take for its real output to double.

The costs of economic growth, and the optimum rate of growth.

Some barriers to economic growth.

How taxation and inflation affect economic growth.

FILL-IN QUESTIONS

Complete the following sentences. (Answers are given at the end of the chapter.)

1. Interest which is computed on a principal sum and also on all the interest earned by that principal sum as of a given date is called _____ _____ .

2. _____ states that the number of years it takes for a quantity which is growing at a given compound rate of interest to double is approximately equal to 72 divided by that compound rate.

3. The idea of Joseph Shumpeter that a capitalist economy grows by replacing old methods of production, old sources of supply, and old skills and resources with new ones is called the _____ _____ .

4. When consumers are prevented from spending part of their income, _____ is said to occur.

PROBLEMS

(Answers are given at the end of the chapter.)

1. Assume that an economy has real NNP of $100 and is growing at a compound rate of 4 percent per year.

   (a) Its real NNP at the end of 1 year will be $ _____ ;

   its real NNP at the end of 2 years will be $ _____ ;

   and its real NNP at the end of 3 years will be

   $ _____ .

   (b) It will take about _____ years for its real NNP to double.

   (c) What would its growth rate have to be in order to have its real NNP double in 12 years? _____ percent.

2. Answer the following questions by referring to the growth-rate table in the text:

   (a) If real GNP is $100 and is growing at 6 percent per year, real GNP at the end of 9 years will be

   $ _____ .

   (b) If real GNP is $412 in one year and 10 years later it is $732, it has been growing at a compound rate of about _____ percent per year.

   (c) If an economy tripled its real income in about 28 years, it must have been growing at about _____ percent per year.

SELF-TEST: TRUE–FALSE QUESTIONS

Circle T if the statement is true, F if it is false. (Answers are given at the end of the chapter.)

T F 1. Real GNP has grown in the United States by over 6 percent per year since the turn of the century.

T F 2. Capital deepening has occurred in the United States since the turn of the century, and has been accompanied by real wages rising in relation to the return on capital.

T F 3. On the basis of historical trends, it would appear that the United States would obtain a faster rate of economic growth if investment were directed more toward human capital than toward capital goods.

T F 4. If GNP is growing at 5 percent per year, it would take 72 years for it to double.

T F 5. If real GNP doubles in 6 years, it must be growing at 12 percent per year.

T F 6. If an economy grows over time but the average workweek remains the same, it cannot be said that one cost of this growth is leisure foregone.

T F 7. If, to obtain growth, people forgo $100 of present consumption but receive an additional $120 of income in 5 years over what they would have received had growth not occurred, the sacrifice of present consumption was obviously worth the future gains.

T F 8. Economic insecurity is one result of the process of creative destruction.

T F 9. The optimal rate of growth occurs when the total benefits from growth equal the total costs of growth.

T F 10. An economy will tend to grow more slowly, other things being equal, if its labor force is geographically or technologically immobile.

T F 11. The more the government absorbs the costs of labor mobility, the more efficiently resources will be sued.

T F 12. Money capital, by definition, is always fully mobile.

T F 13. Evidence suggests that the proportion of GNP allocated to personal saving in the United States is likely to fall in the future.

T F 14. If a corporation considers 18 percent as the minimally acceptable rate of return on capital after taxes, to make investment worthwhile it must receive 30 percent before taxes if the tax rate is 40 percent.

T F 15. Whenever prices are rising, forced saving occurs.

T F 16. In a market economy, forced saving is never used to help finance economic growth.

Circle the letter that corresponds to the best answer.
(Answers are given at the end of the chapter.)

1. Since 1900, annual growth of real GNP per capita in the United States has averaged about:
   (a) 0.5 percent.
   (b) 2 percent.
   (c) 4 percent.
   (d) 7 percent.
   (e) 8 percent.

2. Over the years, the share of total output going to labor:
   (a) Has increased markedly.
   (b) Has remained about the same.
   (c) Has decreased markedly.
   (d) Has decreased markedly, but real hourly wages have increased.
   (e) Has remained about the same, as have real hourly wages.

3. Which of the following has contributed most to growth in the United States since 1950?
   (a) An increase in the average workweek.
   (b) An increase in the quantity of capital.
   (c) Improved education and training.
   (d) Improved technology.
   (e) There is no information on this subject.

4. If an economy is growing at 4 percent per year, how many years will it take for its real GNP to double?
   (a) It depends on what real GNP is to start with.
   (b) 72 years.
   (c) 5½ years.
   (d) 328 years.
   (e) 18 years.

5. If real GNP of an economy is $100 and it is growing at 5 percent per year, its real GNP in 3 years will be:
   (a) $110.0.
   (b) $115.0.
   (c) $115.8.
   (d) $118.4.
   (e) There is not enough information to tell.

6. For the economy to grow it may have to sacrifice:
   (a) Leisure.
   (b) Saving.
   (c) Investment.

   (d) Real income.
   (e) All of the above.

7. Which of the following is true of investment?
   (a) The returns to intangible investment are variable.
   (b) Some types of investment have a greater impact on quality of life than on GNP.
   (c) Some types of investment increase GNP but do not contribute to an improvement in the quality of life.
   (d) The degree of present sacrifice required for a given amount of investment is the same, regardless of the type of investment.
   (e) All of the above.

8. The optimum rate of growth is that at which:
   (a) The costs of growth equal the benefits of growth.
   (b) The present value of the costs of growth equal the present value of the benefits of growth.
   (c) The increased costs of more growth equal the increased benefits of more growth.
   (d) The present value of the increased costs of more growth equals the present value of the increased benefits of more growth.
   (e) The benefits of growth exceed the costs of growth by the greatest possible amount.

9. Which of the following does not contribute to labor immobility?
   (a) Ignorance of employment opportunities.
   (b) High costs of moving from one location to another.
   (c) The existing system of seniority privileges.
   (d) High costs of entering new professions.
   (e) Different wage rates in different professions.

10. The larger the stock of capital goods that an economy has:
    (a) The faster it is growing.
    (b) The higher is its capital–output ratio.
    (c) The larger is the amount of resources that it must use to maintain its capital stock.
    (d) The higher its saving rate must be.
    (e) The longer the average workweek must be.

11. An increase in the corporate income tax rate:
    (a) Increases the expected rate of return on investment before taxes.
    (b) Increases the minimum accepted rate of return on investment after taxes.
    (c) Decreases the expected rate of return on investment before taxes.
    (d) Increases the minimum required rate of return on investment before taxes.
    (e) Decreases the minimum accepted rate of return on investment after taxes.

12. Which of the following will *not* tend to cause forced saving?
    (a) A simultaneous and equal increase in money wages and prices.
    (b) Corporations retaining part of their earnings.
    (c) Personal income taxation, where the tax proceeds are used by the government for investment.
    (d) An increase in prices unaccompanied by an increase in wages.
    (e) All of the above tend to cause forced saving.

CHECKPOINT: LEARNING OBJECTIVES

At this point you should be able to do all of the following:

1. Define all of the technical terms and concepts listed at the end of the chapter in the text.

2. Identify the trends in the following variables for the U.S. economy since 1900:
    (a) The amount of capital per worker.
    (b) Real wages and the proportion of total output going to labor.
    (c) The interest rate in relation to real wages.

3. Compare the growth rate of the U.S. economy with the growth rates of other developed economies.

4. Identify, in terms of their relative importance, the factors that have been responsible for U.S. growth, and the trends in these factors.

5. Calculate:
    (a) How long it would take an economy growing at a given rate to double its output.
    (b) The rate of growth of output over a period, given the initial and terminal values of real GNP and the length of the period.

6. Explain briefly the following costs of economic growth:
    (a) The sacrifice of leisure.
    (b) The sacrifice of consumption.
    (c) The sacrifice of the present for the future.
    (d) The sacrifice of environmental quality.
    (e) The sacrifice of security.

7. Explain what is meant by an optimum rate of growth.

8. Discuss the following barriers to economic growth:
    (a) Labor immobility.
    (b) Capital immobility.
    (c) Limitations on the proportion of resources that can be committed to capital goods production.

9. Explain how high marginal tax rates affect saving.

10. Explain how changes in tax rates affect investment.

11. Describe how inflation, taxation, and the retention of profit by corporations tend to cause forced saving.

12. Explain the relationship between inflation and balanced growth.

QUESTIONS TO THINK ABOUT

1. "If two countries are growing at the same rate but at a point in time one has a higher real GNP per capita than the other, the gap between their average standards of living will widen." Is this necessarily true?

2. Who is likely to benefit from economic growth? To be hurt by it?

3. "In an underdeveloped economy, economic development requires forced saving." In what sense, if any, would this statement be correct?

4. "Dollar for dollar, the current costs of growth mean more than the future benefits of growth." Is this true?

5. If you were asked what growth rate the U.S. economy should aim for, what factors would you consider, and how would you go about estimating the optimum growth rate?

6. Congress continuously discusses "tax reform." Given that the government must raise a certain amount of money through taxes, can you think of how taxes might be restructured so as to provide more stimulus to economic growth?

ANSWERS

Answers to Fill-in Questions

1. compound interest
2. The Rule of 72
3. process of creative destruction
4. forced saving

Answers to Problems

1. (a) $104.00
      $108.16
      $112.4864
   (b) 18
   (c) 6

2. (a) $168.90
   (b) 6 percent (slightly less)
   (c) 4 percent

Answers to True–False Questions

1. F
2. T
3. T
4. F
5. T
6. F (People could have had more leisure and less growth.)
7. F
8. T
9. F
10. T
11. F
12. F
13. T
14. T
15. F (Forced saving occurs when prices rise faster than money wages.)
16. F

Answers to Multiple-Choice Questions

1. b
2. b
3. c
4. e
5. c
6. a
7. e
8. d
9. e
10. c
11. d
12. a

CHAPTER 19

Resource Policies: Energy and the Environment

CHAPTER ORIENTATION

This chapter develops and explains the following concepts:

The nature of the basic energy problem faced by all nations.

Different oil and natural gas policies which have been pursued by the United States over the years, and their implications for efficiency and equity.

Some advantages and disadvantages of rationing.

Incentives for demand reduction and supply expansion, which are two means for reducing the dependence of the United States on foreign energy sources.

Several approaches to pollution control, including the levying of emission fees on polluters, sale of "pollution rights," subsidization of pollution-abatement measures, and direct controls.

FILL-IN QUESTIONS

(Answers are given at the end of the chapter.)

1. If at a given price the quantity supplied of a commodity exceeds the quantity demanded, the amount by which the quantity supplied exceeds the quantity demanded is called a _____ .

2. If at a given price the quantity demanded of a commodity exceeds the quantity supplied, the amount by which the quantity demanded exceeds the quantity supplied is called a _____ .

PROBLEMS

(Answers are given at the end of the chapter.)

1. Assume that S and D in the following diagram represent the supply of and demand for a certain type of energy resource in 1935.
   (a) If a regulatory commission permitted the price of the resource to be established at P_1, it would, in fact, have been pursuing (a surplus/a shortage/neither a surplus nor a shortage) _____

   _____

   policy.

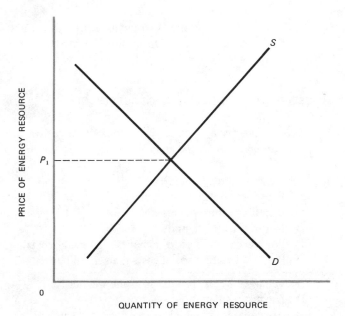

QUANTITY OF ENERGY RESOURCE

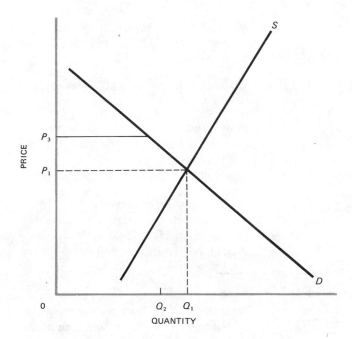

QUANTITY

(b) If over time the demand for the energy resource increased but the supply remained the same, the regulatory commission, by maintaining P_1, would, in fact, be pursuing (a surplus/a shortage/neither a surplus nor a shortage) _____

_____

policy.

(c) If over time the supply of the resource increased but the demand for it did not, then the regulatory commission, by maintaining P_1 would, in fact, be pursuing (a surplus/a shortage/neither a surplus nor a shortage)

_____

_____ policy.

2. In the following diagram S and D represent the free-market supply of and demand for oil during a certain period of time.

(a) Assume that production is restricted to Q_2. Show the price P_2 which is the greatest price that consumers will be willing to pay in order to obtain Q_2. P_2 is (above/below/equal to) _____ the free-market equilibrium price. If P_2 prevails in the market, show on the diagram the potential surplus

that producers would be willing to supply if their output were not restricted.

(b) Show on the diagram the amount of oil that would have to be produced in order to maintain a price equal to P_3 (call it Q_3). Q_3 is (greater than/equal to/less than) _____ the quantity that would be produced if the market were unrestricted.

SELF-TEST: TRUE–FALSE QUESTIONS

Circle T if the statement is true, F if it is false. (Answers are given at the end of the chapter.)

T F 1. The basic energy problem facing the United States is that there are few resources left in the ground to be extracted.

T F 2. If the government establishes a maximum price that may be charged for a commodity, a shortage of that commodity must develop.

T F 3. Output and import quotas on oil tend to hurt consumers and efficient producers, and benefit inefficient small producers.

T F 4. In the early 1970s the United States shifted from a surplus oil policy to a shortage policy.

T F 5. Although export restrictions by OPEC restricted quantity, OPEC had little effect on world oil prices.

T F 6. The wellhead price of "old" gas exceeds that of new gas.

T F 7. Both industrial users and "old" household and commercial users of natural gas have benefited from gas price regulation, whereas "new" household and commercial users have suffered.

T F 8. Because the price of natural gas paid by industrial users is not regulated, industrial purchasers usually face far more serious shortages of natural gas than do residential and commercial users.

T F 9. Rationing tends to discourage investment and to transfer income from consumers of the rationed commodity to government bureaucrats.

T F 10. Oil entitlements are a type of ration coupon which entitle consumers to oil.

T F 11. Conservation means that energy resources must be left in the ground for future generations.

T F 12. One disadvantage of using selective price guarantees to encourage the development of new energy sources is that the government would have to subsidize producers even if the market demand for their product — hence market price — were high.

T F 13. Variable tariffs (which might be used to protect domestic producers from market disruption by oil-exporting countries) tend to have less adverse consequences than import quotas.

T F 14. By levying varying emissions fees on producers, firms would be forced to calculate the cost of their wastes and would be encouraged to consider alternative production and pricing methods.

T F 15. If firms were given tax credits for the purchase of pollution-abatement equipment, they would be encouraged to reduce pollution but not necessarily in the least costly way.

T F 16. Giving tax credits for the purchase of pollution control devices tends to increase the degree to which society's resources are misallocated.

T F 17. Most economists would agree that direct controls on pollution should never be used in a market economy.

SELF-TEST: MULTIPLE-CHOICE QUESTIONS

Circle the answer that corresponds to the best answer. (Answers are given at the end of the chapter.)

1. Government oil regulation has:
   (a) Benefited most consumers.
   (b) Benefited all producers.
   (c) Not benefited anybody.
   (d) Produced greater social benefits than social costs.
   (e) Produced greater social costs than social benefits.

2. Prices charged by gas producers at the wellhead:
   (a) Are not regulated.
   (b) Are equal to marginal costs.
   (c) Depend on whether the gas is defined as "old" or "new."
   (d) Are equal to the average of prices of imported gas.
   (e) Were regulated prior to 1960 but have not been regulated since.

3. Which of the following statements about wellhead gas pricing is *incorrect*?
   (a) By keeping gas prices low, the use of natural gas by residential and commercial customers has increased relative to the use of alternative energy sources.
   (b) Intrastate gas users have been able to obtain all the gas they want at free-market prices.
   (c) By setting wellhead prices below those that would prevail in unrestricted markets, a gas shortage has been created.
   (d) The price of gas to industrial customers has not been regulated.
   (e) The federally imposed price ceilings have discouraged exploration.

4. Which of the following statements about rationing is *incorrect*?
   (a) It would be difficult to determine fairly who should get how much.
   (b) Rationing would increase U.S. dependence on foreign oil, since people could not get as much oil as they want at home.
   (c) Rationing would be necessary only if the regulated price were set below the price that would prevail in the free market.
   (d) The implementation of rationing requires the use of resources and thus produces inefficiencies.

(e) Rationing tends to produce black markets.

5. The oil entitlements program:
   (a) Attempted to allocate relatively cheap "old" oil proportionately among refiners.
   (b) Resulted in a huge waste of resources because enormous amounts of oil were transported between different refiners.
   (c) Encouraged the production of "old" oil by making it more desirable.
   (d) Encouraged and subsidized the importation of oil.
   (e) Increased the profits of refiners, especially large ones.

6. The primary advantage of a free market in energy is that:
   (a) Prices for consumers would be low.
   (b) All persons would share the burdens of changing prices equally and equitably.
   (c) A free market would result in increasing production and would require the economy to adjust to the real cost of energy.
   (d) The demand for energy would not increase over time.
   (e) Conservation would be encouraged because more resources would be left in the ground.

7. One difference between levying fees on polluters and giving subsidies to firms which reduce pollution is that:
   (a) The former would reduce pollution, whereas the latter would not.
   (b) The former places the cost of pollution directly on polluting firms and consumers who purchase their products, whereas the latter spreads the cost to all taxpayers.
   (c) The former would encourage producers to install anti-pollution devices, whereas the latter would not.
   (d) The former would force producers to calculate the cost of their waste disposal, whereas the latter would not.
   (e) The former would affect the profits of firms, whereas the latter would not.

CHECKPOINT: LEARNING OBJECTIVES

At this point, you should be able to:

1. Define all of the technical terms and concepts listed at the end of the chapter in the text.

2. Describe what government legislators would do if they wanted to pursue:
   (a) A free-market policy.
   (b) A surplus policy.
   (c) A shortage policy.

3. Describe U.S. oil policy prior to the early 1970s and state which groups were injured and which benefited from this policy.

4. Describe the shift in policy that occurred in the early 1970s.

5. Explain why government regulation of oil has had adverse effects on both efficiency and equity.

6. Describe the pricing method used by the FPC for the regulation of wellhead gas prices, and explain the objectives of this pricing procedure.

7. Describe why this wellhead pricing policy:
   (a) Resulted in a natural gas shortage.
   (b) Led to increased use of other types of energy by residential and commercial as opposed to industrial customers.
   (c) Benefited intrastate users of gas relative to interstate users.

8. Describe the inefficiencies and inequities that have resulted from federally imposed price ceilings on interstate gas.

9. Describe some pros and cons regarding rationing as a method of dealing with the U.S. energy problem and explain why such a policy would create inefficiencies and inequities.

10. Describe the multilevel price structure for crude oil and the oil entitlements program instituted in the early 1970s, and describe their consequences with regard to efficiency and equity.

11. Explain how high energy prices would encourage conservation, and how selective price guarantees and variable tariffs could be used to encourage the development of new energy sources.

12. Describe the primary advantages and disadvantages of a free market in energy.

13. Discuss the arguments in favor of levying emission fees on polluters, and some rebuttals to these argments.

14. Explain how the sale of "pollution rights" would both reduce pollution and encourage firms that could stop polluting most cheaply to do so.

15. Explain why giving firms tax credits for installing pollution control equipment would be economically less desirable than subsidizing them for pollution reduction.

16. Explain why giving subsidies to firms for pollution abatement violates the benefit principle of equity.

17. Discuss the desirability of direct prohibition of pollution as compared with market-oriented methods of pollution reduction.

QUESTIONS TO THINK ABOUT

1. Whenever the price of a product is regulated, the government, intentionally or not, is pursuing either a surplus or a shortage policy. Why is this so? Is it ever not so?

2. If the price of any one energy source is regulated, can there be efficiency in the production and distribution of any other energy source? Why or why not?

3. Many people argue that the only sensible energy policy for the United States to pursue is complete deregulation and absence of all government interference in the market mechanism. Do you agree with this?

4. "The only way to conserve energy is to impose such a high charge for it that poeple will not want to use it. Thus, only a surplus policy makes sense from a long-run perspective." Is this true?

5. Many people argue that nonreturnable ("one-way") bottles are a serious source of pollution because people throw them away in parks, along roadsides, and so on. What are the advantages and disadvantages of each of the following proposed solutions?
   (a) Prohibiting nonreturnable bottles.
   (b) Taxing companies that produce them.
   (c) Taxing companies that use them to bottle their beverages.
   (d) Taxing consumers who buy them.

6. Would a variable "effluent charge" based on location actually reduce pollution or merely spread it around more evenly? If it would simply spread it around, what benefit, if any, would such a program yield?

7. It might be argued that the sale of "pollution rights" would reduce pollution in the least costly way. In what sense would this be true? If you were in charge of the program, how would you determine the number of "pollution rights" to supply for different kinds of pollution?

8. Would it be possible to use "pollution cleanup" as a countercyclical stabilization device — allow firms to pollute, and have the government spend money to clean up when the economy is slack? Would this be a desirable policy? Why or why not?

Answers to Fill-in Questions

1. surplus
2. shortage

Answers to Problems

1. (a) neither a surplus nor a shortage
   (b) a shortage
   (c) a surplus

2.

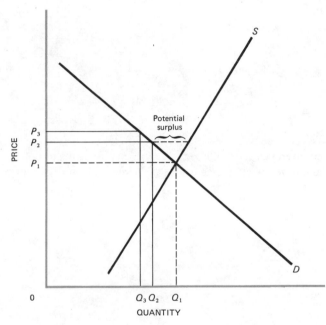

(a) above
(b) less than

Answers to True–False Questions

1. F	9. T
2. F (The price could be above the free-market equilibrium price.)	10. F
	11. F
	12. F
3. T	13. T
4. T	14. T
5. F	15. T
6. F	16. T
7. T	17. F
8. F	

Answers to Multiple-Choice Questions

1. e
2. c
3. a
4. b
5. a
6. c
7. b

PART 5

International Economics, Development, and Planning

CHAPTER 20

International Trade:
Comparative Advantage and Protectionism

CHAPTER ORIENTATION

This chapter develops and explains the following concepts:

That even though U.S. exports and imports comprise a relatively small percentage of its GNP, international trade is still highly significant for the U.S. economy.

That trade occurs because countries are differently suited in the production of different goods as a result of differences in such factors as resource endowments and skills.

That trade between nations can take place even if one country is more efficient in the production of all goods.

That international trade can benefit all countries through more efficient allocation of world resources.

That individual industries may be hurt by free trade, with a consequence that protection has been granted, even in cases where it has been harmful to the economy as a whole.

That tariffs are preferred to quotas with regard to their effects on efficiency, equity, stability, and growth.

That changes in imports and exports have a multiplied effect on national income similar to that caused by changes in other components of aggregate demand.

FILL-IN QUESTIONS

Complete the following sentences. (Answers are given at the end of the chapter.)

1. The _____

   _____

   states that a basis for trade exists between regions when each can provide the other with a good or service for less than it would cost to produce the product at home.

2. When countries engage in specialization and trade, the amount by which a country benefits from trade is called

   _____ .

3. The number of units of a good that must be given up in trade in order to receive one unit of another good is called

   _____ .

4. The _____

   _____

   states that if one nation can produce each of two commodities more efficiently than another nation, and the first nation can produce one of these commodities with relatively greater efficiency than the other commodity, the first nation should specialize in production of the product in which it is most efficient and leave production of the alternative product to the second nation.

5. A tax imposed by a government on the importation or exportation of a good is called a _____ .

6. A(n) _____ places a precise legal limit on the amount of a commodity that may be imported during a given period.

7. A(n) _____ is an underdeveloped industry that may not be able to survive competition from abroad.

8. The _____

_____

is a principle which states that fluctuations in exports or imports may generate magnified variations in national income.

PROBLEM

(Answers are given at the end of the chapter.)

1. Countries X and Y produce the following maximum amounts of cakes *or* hot cross buns with one day's labor and full employment.

	Cakes (dozens)	*or*	Hot cross buns (dozens)
X	1,000		2,000
Y	600		3,000

(a) Country X has a comparative advantage in the production of _____ ,

and Country Y has a comparative advantage in the production of _____ .

(b) Before trade, cakes and hot cross buns should trade in the ratio _____ in Country X and in the ratio _____ in Country Y.

(c) In order for both countries to gain from trade, the price ratio would have to become established at

_____

_____

_____ .

(d) Assume that the countries do not trade, and that each day both X and Y devote a total of half a day's labor to produce cakes and a total of half a day's labor to produce hot cross buns.

Fill in the following table, showing actual daily production of cakes and buns in each country.

Actual Production without Specialization and Trade

	Cakes (dozens)	Hot cross buns (dozens)
X	_____	_____
Y	_____	_____

(e) Now assume that each country specializes in producing that good in which it has a comparative advantage and devotes the entire day's labor to that good.

Fill in the following table, showing actual daily production in each country.

Actual Production with Specialization

	Cakes (dozens)	Hot cross buns (dozens)
X	_____	_____
Y	_____	_____

(f) Fill in the following table, showing the amounts of both cakes and hot cross buns that each country will be able to consume after trade, assuming that they specialize as shown above, that they trade in the ratio of 1 dozen cakes for 3 dozen hot cross buns, and that X exports 400 dozen cakes.

Actual Consumption with Specialization and Trade

	Cakes (dozens)	Hot cross buns (dozens)
X	_____	_____
Y	_____	_____

(g) Compare your answers to (d) and (f), and state what specialization and trade have done for both countries.

_____

_____

_____

(h) Now assume that the terms of trade change to 1 dozen cakes for $3\frac{1}{2}$ dozen hot cross buns, and X exports 400 dozen cakes. After trade, X will be able to consume _____ dozen cakes and _____ dozen hot cross buns, and Y will be able to consume _____ dozen cakes and _____ dozen hot cross buns.

(i) When the terms of trade changed from 1 dozen cakes for 3 dozen hot cross buns to 1 dozen cakes for $3\frac{1}{2}$ dozen hot cross buns, the terms of trade have moved in favor of Country _____ and against Country _____. The change in terms of trade leaves Country _____ better off and Country _____ worse off. Do both countries still gain from trade? _____ In conclusion, a country will gain more from trade, the (more/less) _____ its pretrade price ratio differs from its after-trade price ratio.

SELF-TEST: TRUE–FALSE QUESTIONS

Circle T if the statement is true, F if it is false. (Answers are given at the end of the chapter.)

T F 1. The fundamental questions of WHAT, HOW MUCH, and FOR WHOM apply primarily to domestic analysis, not international economic analysis.

T F 2. Because U.S. imports and exports represent a relatively small fraction of GNP, international trade is for all intents and purposes insignificant for the United States.

T F 3. Since World War II the underdeveloped nations' share of world trade has increased markedly.

T F 4. The industrialized nations constitute the largest markets for our exports.

T F 5. Countries normally specialize in production because they differ in resources, skills, and other endowments.

T F 6. A country may, in fact, export a good in which it does not have an absolute advantage.

T F 7. If one country is extremely efficient in the production of all goods, it will normally export all its goods rather than import.

T F 8. If the relative price ratio of two goods is the same for a country whether or not it engages in international trade, that country will not gain from trade.

T F 9. If an exporter of wheat got two yoyos for each bushel of wheat he exported, and international conditions changed so that he got three yoyos per bushel, the terms of trade would have moved in his favor.

T F 10. If a country is twice as efficient in the production of one good than of another, it will normally export twice as much of it.

T F 11. Everybody benefits from free and unrestricted trade.

T F 12. International trade tends to equalize product and factor prices in trading nations.

T F 13. _Ad valorem_ tariff revenues increase when more units of a good are imported, regardless of the price at which the units are sold.

T F 14. The general level of U.S. tariffs has tended to rise since the early 1800s.

T F 15. Import quotas do not disrupt economic activity as much as tariffs because they do not affect domestic prices.

T F 16. A major problem with the infant-industry argument for tariff protection is that it tends to be applied to industries that in maturity would not be highly efficient and competitive in unrestricted world markets.

T F 17. Normally it would be better to give a subsidy to a domestic industry that a country wanted to protect than to impose a tariff on competing imports.

T F 18. A high-wage country could not export labor-intensive goods.

T F 19. Import quotas tend to be discriminatory.

T F 20. If imports increase by $100, exports will tend to increase by more than $100.

T F 21. If imports increase and exports decrease by the same amount, national income will increase, other things being equal.

SELF-TEST: MULTIPLE-CHOICE QUESTIONS

Circle the letter that corresponds to the best answer. (Answers are given at the end of the chapter.)

1. If Country A is twice as efficient in the production of bread as is Country B and four times as efficient in the production of liver, then:
   (a) A has a comparative advantage in bread.
   (b) A has a comparative advantage in liver.
   (c) A has an absolute advantage and a comparative advantage in both bread and liver.
   (d) B has an absolute advantage in both bread and liver.
   (e) There is not enough information provided to determine which country has a comparative advantage in which good.

2. A country will gain more from trade:
   (a) The more that relative prices after trade differ from relative prices before trade.
   (b) The more it exports in order to import a unit of product.
   (c) The more the terms of trade move against it.
   (d) The more prices rise at home relative to abroad as a consequence of trade.
   (e) The closer it is to full employment.

3. When a country reduces its tariff barriers so that it imports more:
   (a) All trading countries probably will benefit.
   (b) All people in both the importing and exporting countries probably will benefit.
   (c) All people in the importing country probably will benefit.
   (d) Nobody in the exporting country will benefit because they will end up with fewer goods.
   (e) There is no reason to believe that anybody will benefit because if people get more of some goods, they must get less of others.

4. The terms of trade:
   (a) Measure relative prices in the importing country.
   (b) Measure relative prices in the exporting country.
   (c) Measure how many units of goods must be given up for each unit received in trade by a trading country.
   (d) Measure the volume of exports.
   (e) Measure the total volume of trade.

5. Specific tariffs differ from *ad valorem* tariffs in that:
   (a) Specific tariffs apply only to specific goods, whereas *ad valorem* tariffs apply to all goods.
   (b) Specific tariffs are based on the number of units traded, whereas *ad valorem* tariffs are based on the price of units traded.
   (c) Specific tariffs have increased sharply since 1900, whereas *ad valorem* tariffs have fallen.
   (d) Specific tariffs do not affect the prices of imports, whereas *ad valorem* tariffs do.
   (e) Specific tariffs apply only to goods under quota, whereas *ad valorem* tariffs apply to all goods.

6. The infant-industry argument for tariff protection is legitimate whenever:
   (a) The industry involved is small.
   (b) The industry involved produces a new product.
   (c) The industry involved is undergoing rapid technological change.
   (d) The industry involved, once established, will be able to compete effectively in world markets without protection.
   (e) The industry involved faces stiff competition from abroad.

7. Tariffs are a more desirable form of protection than import quotas because:
   (a) Tariffs do not affect domestic prices, whereas quotas do.
   (b) Tariffs do not affect domestic production, whereas quotas do.
   (c) Tariffs cause less resource misallocation, because the volume of imports remains flexible with tariffs but does not with quotas.
   (d) Tariffs do not impede economic growth, whereas quotas do.
   (e) Tariffs do not affect income distribution, whereas quotas do.

8. An increase in imports not accompanied by a reduction in saving has the same effect on national income, other things being equal, as:
   (a) An equal increase in investment.
   (b) An equal increase in government spending.
   (c) An equal increase in taxes.
   (d) An equal reduction in government spending on domestically produced goods.
   (e) An equal increase in exports.

CHECKPOINT: LEARNING OBJECTIVES

At this point you should be able to do all of the following:

1. Define all of the technical terms and concepts listed at the end of the chapter in the text.

2. Describe the fraction of U.S. GNP which is exported, and compare this with other industrialized countries.

3. Describe the general types of goods that comprise the largest share of U.S. exports, and state the type of countries to which most of our exports go.

4. Given the amounts of two products that two countries could produce with one day's labor at full employment, state:
   (a) Which country, if either, has a comparative advantage in the production of which good.
   (b) The price ratios of the two goods in each country in the absence of trade.
   (c) What price ratio for trade will make both countries better off.

5. Describe why countries have absolute and comparative advantages in the production of different products.

6. Explain what is meant by the terms of trade moving in favor of or against a trading nation.

7. Explain how tariffs and quotas affect:
   (a) The allocation of world resources.
   (b) The consumers' freedom of choice.

8. Explain each of the following arguments for protection, state the conditions, if any, under which each is valid, and discuss the shortcomings each may have:
   (a) The infant-industry argument.
   (b) The national-security argument.
   (c) The diversified-economy argument.
   (d) The wage-protection argument.
   (e) The employment-protection argument.

9. Explain why tariffs are preferred to quotas with regard to their effects on efficiency, equity, stability, and growth.

10. Explain why changes in imports and exports produce multiplied changes in an economy's output and employment.

QUESTIONS TO THINK ABOUT

1. The cry is frequently heard in less developed nations for protection from "efficient American labor." What would prompt this? Is the logic underlying this any different from the logic underlying the cry heard in the United States for protection from cheap foreign labor?

2. During the Great Depression countries attempted to use tariffs in order to "export unemployment." How would this work?

3. "A major problem with using tariffs to provide revenues for the government is that the more you raise tariffs, the less revenue you will get." Under what circumstances, if any, is this statement true?

4. Whether a country exports or imports depends on both efficiency in production and the cost of labor and other factor services. Explain carefully what part each plays.

5. "The major problem with imposing tariffs is that, as history has shown, other countries will retaliate, so that you end up no better off than you were before." Do you agree?

6. In reality, as production increases, costs tend to rise. Therefore, if a country increases production for export, prices of exported products will rise. Does this affect the free-trade argument?

ANSWERS

Answers to Fill-in Questions

1. law of absolute advantage
2. the gains from trade
3. the terms of trade
4. law of comparative advantage
5. tariff
6. import quota
7. infant industry
8. foreign-trade multiplier

Answers to Problem

1. (a) cakes
   hot cross buns
   (b) 1:2
   1:5
   (c) between 1 dozen cakes for 2 dozen hot cross buns and 1 dozen cakes for 5 dozen hot cross buns

(d)

	Cakes (dozens)	Hot cross buns (dozens)
X	500	1,000
Y	300	1,500

(e)

	Cakes (dozens)	Hot cross buns (dozens)
X	1,000	0
Y	0	3,000

(f)

	Cakes (dozens)	Hot cross buns (dozens)
X	600	1,200
Y	400	1,800

(g) Specialization and trade have enabled both countries to consume more of both goods.

(h) 600
    1,400
    400
    1,600
(i) X
    Y
    X
    Y
    Yes
    more

Answers to True–False Questions

1. F		12. T
2. F		13. F
3. F		14. F
4. T		15. F
5. T		16. T
6. T		17. T
7. F		18. F
8. T		19. T
9. T		20. F
10. F		21. F (See the macroeconomics section of the text.)
11. F		

Answers to Multiple-Choice Questions

1. b	5. b
2. a	6. d
3. a	7. c
4. c	8. d

CHAPTER 21

International Finance:
Exchange Rates and the Balance of Payments

CHAPTER ORIENTATION

This chapter develops and explains the following concepts:

The nature and functions of foreign exchange markets.

The nature of the balance-of-payments statement and balance-of-payments accounts as a system of double-entry bookkeeping.

The meaning of equilibrium in the balance of payments.

How a system of freely floating exchange rates would operate to prevent sustained disequilibrium in the balance of payments.

How modern economics can correct balance-of-payments disequilibrium through price and income changes or through direct controls.

How in theory the gold standard would operate and prevent sustained external disequilibrium.

FILL-IN QUESTIONS

Complete the following sentences. (Answers are given at the end of the chapter.)

1. The instruments used to make international payments are called _____.

2. A statement of the money value of all transactions between a nation and the rest of the world during a given period is called a _____

   _____.

3. In balance-of-payments accounting, any transaction that results in a money outflow or payment to a foreign country is called a _____, and any transaction that results in a money inflow or receipt from a foreign country is called a _____.

4. The part of a nation's balance of payments dealing with the relationship between the export and import of goods is called the _____

   _____.

5. _____ transactions are those which are undertaken for reasons that are independent of the balance of payments, while _____

_____ transactions are those which are undertaken as a direct response to balance-of-payments considerations.

6. When over a period of time the sum of a country's autonomous debits does not equal the sum of its autonomous credits, the country is said to have a _____

_____

_____ .

7. The price of one currency in terms of another is called the

_____ .

8. The upper and lower limits within which the foreign exchange rates of gold standard countries could fluctuate were called the _____ .

PROBLEM

(Answers are given at the end of the chapter.)

1. Assume that exchange rates are free to fluctuate and that people in the United States want to import a good from Great Britain that costs £1 per unit.

   (a) Given the foreign price of the good, calculate its U.S. price at different exchange rates, and enter this in column (3).

(1) Exchange rate ($/£)	(2) Foreign price of good	(3) U.S. price of good	(4) Quantity demanded	(5) Total desired expenditures in £s
2.00/1	£1	$_____	100	£_____
2.20/1	1	_____	90	_____
2.40/1	1	_____	80	_____
2.60/1	1	_____	70	_____
2.80/1	1	_____	60	_____

   Thus, as the dollar price of pounds rises, the dollar price of the good (rises/remains the same/falls)

   _____ .

   (b) Given the quantity of the good demanded at different prices, calculate the amount of *pounds* that people in the United States want to spend on the good at different dollar prices, and enter this in column (5). Column (5) is the _____ for pounds at different exchange rates. Graph this in the space provided.

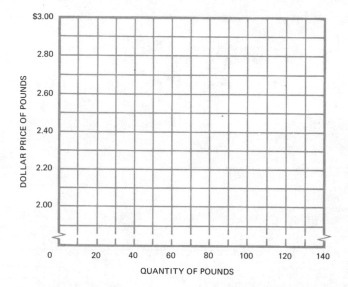

   (c) Now assume that people in Great Britain want to import a good from the United States which costs $1 per unit.

(6) Exchange rate ($/£)	(7) Dollar price of good	(8) Pound price of good	(9) Quantity demanded	(10) Total desired expenditures in £s
2.00/1	$1	£_____	120	£_____
2.20/1	1	_____	156	_____
2.40/1	1	_____	190	_____
2.60/1	1	_____	237	_____
2.80/1	1	_____	278	_____

   Given the dollar price of the good, calculate its price in pounds at different exchange rates and enter this in column (8). As the dollar price of the pound rises, the pound price of the good (rises/remains the same/falls)

   _____ .

   (d) Given the quantity of the good demanded at different (pound) prices, calculate the amount of *pounds* that people in Great Britain want to spend on the good at different pound prices, and enter this in column (10). Column (10) is the _____ of pounds at different exchange rates. Put this on the graph given in (b).

(e) If the only international trade between these countries involves that in the two goods above, the equilibrium exchange rate will be approximately _____ $/£ or _____ £/$.

(f) Now assume that the U.S. demand for the British good increases to what is shown in the following table. Enter the total desired expenditures in pounds in this table, and put the new demand for pounds in the graph in (b), labeling it D'.

Exchange rate ($/£)	Pound price of good	Quantity demanded	Total desired expenditures in £s
2.00/1	£1	120	£_____
2.20/1	1	110	_____
2.40/1	1	100	_____
2.60/1	1	90	_____
2.80/1	1	80	_____

The equilibrium exchange rate will become approximately _____ $/£ or _____ £/$. Thus, the increase in U.S. demand for British goods, other things remaining the same, will _____ the dollar price of pounds and _____ the pound price of dollars.

(g) After demand changed, the U.S. will export approximately _____ units of goods to Great Britain, whereas before demand changed, it exported approximately _____ units. After demand changed, the U.S. will import approximately _____ units of goods from Great Britain, whereas before demand changed, it imported approximately _____ units. Thus, U.S. exports (rise/fall) _____, and U.S. imports (rise/fall) _____. After demand changed, total receipts from sale to Great Britain (in dollars) will

equal $ _____, whereas before demand changed, they were $ _____. After demand changed, total expenditures on British goods (in dollars) will equal $ _____, whereas before demand changed, they were $ _____. Hence, the U.S. balance of payments (was/was not) _____ in equilibrium before demand changed and (is/is not) _____ in equilibrium after demand changed.

(h) Finally, assume that the exchange rate was fixed at $2.40/£. When U.S. demand for British goods increased, the United States would have bought _____ units and paid a total of $ _____ for British imports. The British would have bought _____ units from the United States and paid a total of $ _____ for U.S. exports. Thus, the United States would have (lost/gained) _____ _____ $ _____ or £ _____ in foreign exchange.

SELF-TEST: TRUE–FALSE QUESTIONS

Circle T if the statement is true, F if it is false. (Answers are given at the end of the chapter.)

T F   1. In international trade, importers usually pay for the merchandise they buy in their domestic currency, and exporters usually get paid in their domestic currency.

T F   2. An export transaction usually increases the money supply in the exporting country.

T F   3. Because importing requires foreign exchange, a nation can import goods equal to but not exceeding the value of goods that it exports during any particular period of time.

T F   4. If the current, unilateral transfer, and official reserve transaction accounts are in balance, the capital account must be in balance as well.

T F   5. Investing in a business firm in Europe is an autonomous transaction with regard to the balance of payments.

T F 6. Short-term capital flows are often compensatory transactions.

T F 7. If France sells U.S. dollars to West Germany, the U.S. balance of payments is unaffected.

T F 8. A surplus in the balance of payments can occur only when exports of goods and services exceed imports of goods and services.

T F 9. If a nation experiences compensatory transactions over a given period of time, by definition it must have a balance-of-payments imbalance.

T F 10. A country has a balance-of-payments problem unless each year its balance of payments is in exact balance.

T F 11. Under a system of freely fluctuating exchange rates, an increase in the demand for U.S. dollars by Great Britain will cause the pound price of dollars to rise.

T F 12. If the dollar price of marks falls, U.S. imports of German goods should be expected to fall, other things being equal.

T F 13. If a country is experiencing a deficit in its balance of payments, it should encourage deflation, a reduction in income, and/or an increase in the foreign price of its currency.

T F 14. One advantage of freely fluctuating exchange rates is that exports and imports can fluctuate to bring about balance-of-payments equilibrium without having any effect on the domestic economy.

T F 15. Monetary and fiscal policy measures undertaken to correct a balance-of-payments deficit tend to stimulate employment in the domestic economy.

T F 16. The gold export point is defined as the point at which, under the gold standard, it is cheaper to export gold and buy foreign currency abroad than to buy it domestically in the foreign exchange market.

T F 17. If a country under the gold standard does not permit its money supply to fluctuate according to whether gold is being imported or exported, the classical equilibration process will not take place when the country experiences an imbalance in its balance of payments.

T F 18. The par exchange rate between two currencies under the gold standard is not determined by supply and demand.

T F 19. If a country practices exchange controls, it will not normally allow the allocation of foreign exchange to be determined by market forces.

T F 20. Trade controls are better than exchange controls in the sense that they do not interfere with market forces.

SELF-TEST: MULTIPLE-CHOICE QUESTIONS

Circle the letter that corresponds to the best answer.
(Answers are given at the end of the chapter.)

1. Which of the following would not be traded in the foreign exchange markets?
   (a) U.S. dollars.
   (b) British pounds.
   (c) Drafts.
   (d) Time deposits.
   (e) Bills of exchange.

2. Which of the following does *not* occur as a result of international transactions?
   (a) The supply of money in importing countries increases.
   (b) Efficiency in the utilization of world resources increases.
   (c) Exporting countries obtain foreign exchange which they use to pay for imports.
   (d) National income rises in countries whose trade balance becomes more favorable, other things being equal.
   (e) Consumer choice is broadened.

3. Which of the following is *not* an account in the balance-of-payments statement?
   (a) The official reserve transaction account.
   (b) The capital account.
   (c) The debit and credit account.
   (d) The unilateral transfer account.
   (e) The current account.

4. If a country runs a deficit in its balance of payments, it must be true that:
   (a) Its exports exceed its imports.
   (b) Its imports exceed its exports.
   (c) A compensatory capital or international reserve outflow is taking place.
   (d) It is exporting gold.
   (e) It must be giving away too much under its unilateral transfer account.

5. The difference between autonomous and compensatory transactions is that:
   (a) Compensatory transactions are a result of other international transactions, whereas autonomous transactions are undertaken for reasons independent of the balance of payments.
   (b) Compensatory transactions occur in response to unilateral transfers, whereas autonomous transactions never involve unilateral transfers.
   (c) Compensatory transactions frequently involve long-term capital movements, whereas autonomous transactions more frequently involve short-term capital movements.
   (d) Compensatory transactions never involve gold movements, whereas autonomous transactions frequently do.
   (e) Compensatory transactions appear in the balance of payments, whereas autonomous transactions do not.

6. The balance of payments must be in equilibrium whenever:
   (a) The balance of trade is in equilibrium.
   (b) Imbalance in the balance of trade is compensated for by capital movements.
   (c) Debits equal credits.
   (d) No official reserve asset movements occur.
   (e) The sum of autonomous debits equals the sum of autonomous credits.

7. If a country wanted to correct a deficit in its balance of payments, which of the following policy actions would *not* be appropriate (ignoring the other effects and implications of such policy actions)?
   (a) Depreciation of its currency (that is, making it cheaper in terms of other currencies).
   (b) A reduction in taxes.
   (c) A reduction in government spending.
   (d) Deflationary monetary policy.
   (e) Imposing direct controls on imports.

8. Under a system of freely fluctuating exchange rates, if Great Britain's demand for imports from the United States increased, other things being equal:
   (a) Great Britain would have to increase its merchandise exports to the United States.
   (b) Great Britain would have to increase its long-term capital inflows from the United States.
   (c) The British price of U.S. dollars would rise.
   (d) The British price of U.S. dollars would rise to the gold export point and then level off.
   (e) Great Britain would have to export gold.

9. Which of the following is *not* true under a system of freely fluctuating exchange rates?

   (a) Disequilibrium in the balance of payments is automatically corrected.
   (b) Fluctuations in the exchange rate permit balance-of-payments adjustments without having any effect, either direct or indirect, on domestic economies.
   (c) The risk of foreign trade is greater than it would be if exchange rates were fixed.
   (d) The prices of imports and exports change as the supply and demand for foreign exchange changes.
   (e) A country's exchange rate will tend to change as its level of economic activity changes.

10. Under the gold standard (in theory):
    (a) The exchange rate between two currencies never deviates from the par rate.
    (b) A nation's money supply is linked to the volume of its international transactions.
    (c) There is no mechanism for correcting balance-of-payments disequilibria.
    (d) The par rate of exchange is determined by supply and demand.
    (e) A country's exports must equal its imports.

11. Which of the following is *not* true if a country has exchange controls?
    (a) Goods which on the basis of comparative advantage should be imported are frequently produced domestically.
    (b) Black markets tend to prosper.
    (c) Foreign exchange usually sells at different rates for different uses.
    (d) The government often buys all exchange earned in trade and sells it to importers.
    (e) The order of priority for imports is determined strictly by supply and demand.

CHECKPOINT: LEARNING OBJECTIVES

At this point you should be able to do all of the following:

1. Define all of the technical terms and concepts listed at the end of the chapter in the text.

2. Define the most important function of foreign exchange markets.

3. Explain how international trade:
   (a) Increases the supply of money in an exporting country and reduces it in an importing country.
   (b) Provides an exporting country with the foreign exchange which it may use to purchase goods and services from other countries.

4. List the major items included in each of the following balance-of-payments accounts:
   (a) Current account.
   (b) Capital account.
   (c) Unilateral transfer account.
   (d) Official reserve transaction account.

5. Explain why a balance of payments always balances in an accounting sense.

6. Explain why a balance of payments normally includes both autonomous and compensatory items, and state in which accounts (current, capital, unilateral transfer, official reserve transaction) the compensatory items are normally found.

7. Describe the ways in which a country can finance a balance-of-payments deficit.

8. Explain how freely fluctuating exchange rates:
   (a) Automatically correct a disequilibrium in the balance of payments.
   (b) Influence the price that people must pay for imported goods.
   (c) Affect the risk to which parties to international transactions commit themselves.
   (d) Affect the terms of trade of a nation whose currency is depreciated.
   (e) Influence export industries, and thus income and employment.

9. Describe how balance-of-payments disequilibria may be corrected through domestic price and income changes, and how these changes can be brought about.

10. Explain how exchange rates were determined under the gold standard, and why the gold points established the range within which the foreign exchange rates of gold standard currencies fluctuated.

11. Describe how balance-of-payments disequilibria are, in theory, corrected under the gold standard.

12. Explain why exchange controls usually require that the government rather than the free market decide which goods will be imported.

13. Explain why countries use exchange controls, and why these controls:
    (a) Affect the price level in countries imposing them.
    (b) Encourage the development of a black market.
    (c) Encourage retaliatory measures by other countries.

QUESTIONS TO THINK ABOUT

1. Is there any real difference between international and intranational trade other than the fact that in international trade different currencies are used, whereas in intranational trade only one currency is used?

2. How could you explain the fact that immediately after World War II the United States had a very favorable balance of trade but that this has deteriorated sharply since then?

3. Does the distinction between autonomous and compensatory transactions have any significance for policy purposes? If so, what is it?

4. The gold standard worked well in theory but not in practice because there was a tendency for countries running deficits to tighten credit and attract capital rather than lose gold. Explain what the effect of this policy would be on the operation of the gold standard.

5. "A system of freely fluctuating exchange rates is advantageous in that it permits governments to stabilize their economies domestically and not worry about external balance." Do you agree?

6. If in a system of freely fluctuating exchange rates the supply of and demand for foreign exchange were highly interest-inelastic, what would happen to exchange rates as supply and demand changed? What influence would this have on domestic economies?

ANSWERS

Answers to Fill-in Questions

1. foreign exchange
2. balance of payments
3. debit
   credit
4. balance of trade
5. Autonomous
   compensatory
6. balance-of-payments
   disequilibrium
7. foreign exchange rate
8. gold points

Answers to Problem

1. (a)

U.S. price of the good
$2.00
2.20
2.40
2.60
2.80

rises

(b)

Total desired expenditures in £s
£100
90
80
70
60

demand

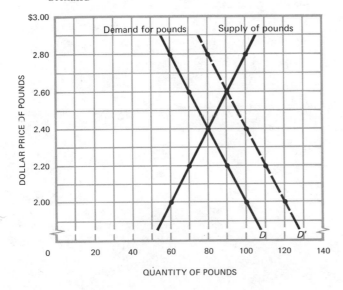

(c)

Pound price of good
£.50
.45
.42
.38
.36

falls

(d)

Total desired expenditures in £s
£ 60.0
70.2
79.8
90.1
100.1

supply

(e) 2.40
     0.42

(f)

Total desired expenditures in £s
£120
110
100
90
80

2.60
0.38
raise
lower

(g) 237
     190
     90
     80
     rise
     rise
     $237
     $190
     $234
     $192
     was
     is

Note: The numbers do not come out exactly because exchange rates of 2.40 and 2.60 $/£ are approximations and quantities are approximations as well. For example, 2.40 $/£ is actually 0.41666 , , , £/$, not 0.42 £/$.

At this rate, the quantity of pounds supplied before demand changed was 79.17 (190 × $0.416667), and the quantity demanded was 80. Therefore, the equilibrium exchange rate must have been slightly higher than 2.40 $/£. If we had the exact equilibrium exchange rate, the (dollar or pound) value of exports would equal the (dollar or pound) value of imports both before and after demand changed.

(h)   100
      $240
      190
      $190
      lost
      $50
      £20.83

Answers to True–False Questions

1.	T	8	F	15.	F
2.	T	9.	T	16.	T
3.	F	10.	F	17.	T
4.	T	11.	T	18.	T
5.	T	12.	F	19.	T
6.	T	13.	F	20.	F
7.	T	14.	F		

Answers to Multiple-Choice Questions

1.	d	5.	a	9.	b
2.	a	6.	e	10.	b
3.	c	7.	b	11.	e
4.	c	8.	c		

CHAPTER 22

International Economic Problems and Policies

CHAPTER ORIENTATION

This chapter develops and explains the following concepts:

The weakening and disintegration of the world economy during the interwar period, and the quest for greater domestic as opposed to international stability during this period.

The recovery of the European nations from World War II with the aid of the European Recovery Program and, later, the Mutual Security Administration.

The attempt to liberalize and expand trade after World War II through the creation of the General Agreement on Trade and Tariffs (GATT) in 1947, other trade-expansion acts, and regional integration in the form of free-trade areas, customs unions, and common markets.

The attempt to create a viable international monetary system through the International Monetary Fund (IMF), and why the system of fixed exchange rates eventually broke down.

Attempts to avoid persisting financial crises through the creation of IMF Special Drawing Rights, and the development of a two-tier system for gold.

Floating, adjustable, and crawling exchange rates, which are three different methods of exchange rate determination.

FILL-IN QUESTIONS

Complete the following sentences. (Answers are given at the end of the chapter.)

1. A _____ standard exists when gold does not circulate domestically as money but is made available for industrial use and international transactions in return for other money.

2. _____ is an official act which makes a domestic currency cheaper in terms of gold or foreign currencies.

3. The _____

_____ program is a plan for expanding U.S. exports through legislation which authorizes the president of the United States to negotiate tariff reductions with other nations in return for parallel concessions. Under it, the _____

_____ requires each signatory to extend to all others the same preferential tariff and trade concessions that it may, in the future, extend to nonsignatories.

4. The _____

_____ was a comprehensive plan, financed by the United States for the economic revitalization of European nations after World War II.

5. The _____ is an international agreement signed in 1947 by 23 countries in an attempt to achieve nondiscrimination in trade, tariff reduction, the elimination of import quotas, and resolution of differences through consultation.

6. An association of trading nations whose participants agree to impose no restrictive devices such as tariffs and quotas on one another, although each is free to impose whatever restrictions it wishes on nonparticipants, is called a _____; an agreement among trading nations to abolish trade barriers among themselves and to adopt a common external trade policy with all nonmember nations is a _____

_____;

and an association of trading nations whose participants agree to impose no trade restrictions among themselves, establish common external barriers to nonparticipants, and impose no national restrictions on the movement of labor and capital between them is called a _____

_____.

7. The _____

_____

is an organization established in 1944 for the purposes of eliminating exchange controls, providing for the worldwide convertability of currencies and stabilizing exchange rates.

8. Supplementary reserves, established in 1969, in the form of account entries on the books of the IMF are called _____

_____.

9. Under a system of _____

_____,

exchange rates are determined by the interaction of supply and demand, under a(n) _____

_____ system, small changes in exchange rates are permitted if a nation has a short-run balance-of-payments disequilibrium; and under a(n) _____ system, changes in a nation's exchange rate occur automatically by small increments if in actual daily trading on the foreign exchange markets, the price of its currency persists on the "floor" or "ceiling" of the established range for a period of time.

10. _____ are dollar accounts held in foreign banks all over the world.

11. _____ is foreign exchange which is bought (or sold) at a given time and at a stipulated price, but is payable at some future date.

SELF-TEST: TRUE—FALSE QUESTIONS

Circle T if the statement is true, F if it is false. (Answers are given at the end of the chapter.)

T F 1. The gold standard which was abandoned during World War I was finally reestablished when the IMF was created.

T F 2. The goal of domestic as opposed to international economic stability became increasingly emphasized after World War I.

T F 3. The Smoot-Hawley Tariff Act of 1930 permitted tariff reductions in order to expand world trade and provide for international economic stability.

T F 4. U.S. devaluation of the dollar in 1934 made U.S. exports cheaper and imports more expensive vis-à-vis the rest of the world.

T F 5. It has been shown historically that devaluation by a country is usually met by retaliatory measures of other nations.

T F 6. The GATT provided international monetary reform so that trade would not be encumbered by international financial restrictions.

T F 7. A common market is another name for a customs union.

T F 8. Formation of a common market among trading countries typically eliminates all trading barriers between the common market countries and the rest of the world.

T F 9. The various acts which are part of the U.S. Reciprocal Trade Agreements program have succeeded in eliminating virtually all tariff barriers between the United States and the rest of the world.

T F 10. The IMF required exchange rate revaluation whenever a country ran a balance-of-payments deficit or surplus.

T F 11. The expansion in European productive potential since the immediate postwar years has been one factor causing the change from a dollar shortage to a dollar surplus.

T F 12. SDRs consist of national currencies other than those of the United States and Great Britain.

T F 13. Devaluation such as that undertaken by Great Britain in 1967 would not have been necessary if the IMF had functioned as it was supposed to.

T F 14. The two-tier system for gold permitted the official price of gold to fluctuate on the basis of free-market forces.

T F 15. The Bretton Woods system placed the burden of international adjustment directly on the discretionary policies of nations.

T F 16. In August, 1971, the United States ended its policy of exchanging dollars held by foreign central banks for gold.

T F 17. Since the early 1970s, exchange rates have tended to be established by a "dirty" float.

T F 18. Eurodollars are deposits of U.S. dollars in banks outside the United States.

T F 19. A major disadvantage of floating exchange rates is that they may encourage speculation in foreign exchange.

T F 20. A "crawling peg" provides more continuous exchange rate adjustment than does a system of freely fluctuating exchange rates.

T F 21. Forward exchange is foreign exchange bought at a given time but payable some time in the future.

T F 22. If a nation's exchange rate is established under an adjustable peg, disruptive currency speculation would never occur as long as people acted rationally.

SELF-TEST: MULTIPLE-CHOICE QUESTIONS

Circle the letter that corresponds to the best answer. (Answers are given at the end of the chapter.)

1. Which of the following was *not* one of the essential features of the international economy prior to World War I?
   (a) Most major nations were on a system of flexible exchange rates which provided for automatic adjustment of balance-of-payments disequilibrium.
   (b) Nations tended to specialize on the basis of their factor endowments.
   (c) Tariffs were of only moderate significance.
   (d) London was the center of finance and trade.
   (e) Nations tended to trade on the basis of comparative advantage.

2. During the 1920s:
   (a) Restoration of the gold standard became a major objective of international policy.
   (b) Countries agreed that it would be undesirable to go back to the gold standard because it imposed too heavy a burden on domestic economic stability.
   (c) The IMF was established to restore international financial equilibrium.
   (d) Most countries remained on an inconvertible paper standard.
   (e) The U.S. dollar and the German mark became key currencies.

3. Which of the following did *not* characterize the 1930s?
   (a) Increased tariff barriers.
   (b) Financial crises.
   (c) Abandonment of gold.
   (d) IMF measures to provide more monetary stability.
   (e) Devaluation of the dollar.

4. Immediately prior to World War II most countries:
   (a) Had returned to the pre-1914 gold standard.
   (b) Had joined the IMF.
   (c) Had agreed to exchange rate stabilization with gold used as an equilibrating device for balance-of-payments purposes.
   (d) Had adopted floating exchange rates.
   (e) Had totally inconvertible currencies.

5. The most-favored-nation clause of the Reciprocal Trade Agreements Act of 1934:
   (a) Granted to all signatories the same preferential tariff and trade concessions that each would extend in the future to nonsignatories.
   (b) Granted to all signatories preferred treatment over nonsignatories.
   (c) Granted the United States preferential treatment with regard to other signatories.
   (d) Assured all signatories that tariffs would not be reduced for nonsignatories.
   (e) Granted to nonsignatories preferential tariff treatment on certain commodities.

6. Which of the following factors was *not* responsible for the European trade deficit after World War II?
   (a) Inflation.
   (b) U.S. devaluation.
   (c) Lost plant capacity.
   (d) Lost export markets.
   (e) Lost manpower.

7. Which of the following was *not* one of the purposes of the Marshall Plan?
   (a) To increase the productive capacity of the European economies.
   (b) To stabilize the financial systems of the European economies.
   (c) To promote mutual economic cooperation.
   (d) To reduce the dependence of European economies on U.S. assistance.
   (e) To develop common markets or free-trade areas among the European economies.

8. Which of the following is *not* a basic principle of the GATT?
   (a) Elimination of the most-favored nation treatment.
   (b) Nondiscrimination in trade.
   (c) Tariff reduction.
   (d) Elimination of import quotas.
   (e) Resolution of differences through consultation.

9. According to the original provisions of the IMF:
   (a) All currencies were to be convertible into gold.
   (b) Exchange rates were to be determined by a "dirty" float.
   (c) All countries were to return to the prewar gold standard.
   (d) Exchange rates for currencies of member countries were to be fixed in relation to the dollar.
   (e) All currencies were to be directly convertible into either gold or SDRs.

10. Which of the following did *not* occur in the 1960s in an attempt to ease the U.S. balance-of-payments problem?
    (a) Domestic deflation.
    (b) Imposition of an interest equalization tax.
    (c) Reduction in the amount of duty-free goods which American tourists could bring back to the United States.
    (d) A request by the United States that European countries carry a larger share of the mutual defense burden.
    (e) A request by the United States that restrictions against U.S. exports be lifted.

11. Special Drawing Rights:
    (a) Are foreign currencies which IMF countries may borrow.
    (b) Have replaced all foreign currencies as international reserves.
    (c) Are supplementary international reserves.
    (d) Prevent countries from having balance-of-payments disequilibria.
    (e) Are expected to prevent dollar deficits in the future.

12. The two-tier system for gold:
    (a) Reduced the dependence of the world economy on the U.S. dollar.
    (b) Substituted paper gold for gold as international reserves.
    (c) Removed the necessity of the Gold Pool countries defending the price of gold in world markets.
    (d) Allowed the official price of gold to be determined by the basic forces of supply and demand.
    (e) Eliminated speculation in gold.

13. Which of the following is *not* true with regard to floating exchange rates?
    (a) They have the advantage of not requiring countries to hold substantial amounts of international reserves.
    (b) They have the advantage of adjusting automatically to encourage balance-of-payments equilibrium.
    (c) They have the advantage of stabilizing the balance of trade.
    (d) They have the disadvantage of increasing uncertainty on the part of importers and exporters.
    (e) They have the disadvantage of encouraging speculation.

14. Under a crawling peg system:
    (a) The exchange rate rises whenever the demand for foreign exchange exceeds supply.
    (b) The exchange rate rises whenever the supply of foreign exchange exceeds demand.
    (c) The exchange rate is adjusted only after a long-run disequilibrium in the balance of payments.

(d) The exchange rate would change automatically by small increments if in actual daily trading it persisted on the floor or ceiling for a specified period of time.

(e) The exchange rate would change automatically by relatively small amounts if in actual daily trading there were either an excess or deficiency of foreign exchange.

CHECKPOINT: LEARNING OBJECTIVES

At this point you should be able to do all the following:

1. Define all of the technical terms and concepts listed at the end of the chapter in the text.

2. Describe, with regard to trading nations prior to World War I:
   (a) The basis for specialization in production.
   (b) The influence of tariffs on trade.
   (c) The nature of the international financial system.

3. Explain how changes in national objectives and increased government intervention in international trade weakened the international monetary mechanism that was established after World War I.

4. Describe briefly the disintegration of the world economy during the early 1930s, including the events that led to the U.S. devaluation in 1934.

5. Explain how other countries responded to the U.S. devaluation, and describe the nature of the financial agreement reached by democratic nations in order to find a compromise between the rigidities of the gold standard and domestic currency management.

6. Discuss the purpose of the Reciprocal Trade Agreements program.

7. Discuss the purposes of the Marshall Plan and the Mutual Security Administration, and state whether or not their results have been favorable.

8. State the four basic principles underlying the GATT.

9. Distinguish between a free-trade area, a customs union, and a common market, and discuss the favorable and unfavorable economic effects of a common market.

10. Describe the powers that the trade agreements acts under the Reciprocal Trade Agreements program gave to the president of the United States.

11. Describe the objectives of the IMF.

12. Describe the nature and degree of success of the policies which the United States undertook in the early 1960s to cope with its balance-of-payments deficit.

13. Explain why speculative flows of funds into and out of different currencies occurred during the 1960s.

14. Explain the purpose of SDRs.

15. Discuss the events leading up to the establishment of a two-tier system for gold, and how this system worked.

16. Describe the actions taken by the United States in the early 1970s to help relieve its international financial problems, and state how exchange rates have been determined since then.

17. Explain why, under the Bretton Woods system, a deficit or surplus in a country's balance of payments was not automatically corrected.

18. Discuss some advantages and disadvantages of each of the following methods of exchange rate determination:
   (a) Floating exchange rates.
   (b) Adjustable pegs.
   (c) Crawling pegs.

QUESTIONS TO THINK ABOUT

1. Should the fact that the dollar is a key currency have influenced the decision of the United States regarding devaluation of the dollar?

2. What effect would there be, if any, on domestic industry if a country which had fixed exchange rates changed to floating exchange rates? Answer explicitly for both export industries and industries that are not already heavily involved in international trade.

3. Would there be any real difference between floating, adjustable, and crawling exchange rates with regard to the impact of international trade on an economy?

4. When the United States devalued the dollar, who benefited most? Who was hurt most?

5. While the United States was running a trade deficit during the second half of the 1960s and the early 1970s, it was also experiencing a substantial inflation. What policy mix could have been used to alleviate both? What reasons can you give for why a better resolution of these two problems was not achieved?

6. How did a two-tier system for gold "take the pressure off" the U.S. dollar?

7. What is the real significance for the United States of SDRs?

ANSWERS

Answers to Fill-in Questions

1. gold bullion
2. Devaluation
3. Reciprocal Trade Agreements
   most-favored nation clause
4. European Recovery Program (Marshall Plan)
5. GATT (General Agreement on Tariffs and Trade)
6. free-trade area
   customs union
   common market
7. International Monetary Fund
8. Special Drawing Rights
9. floating exchange rates
   adjustable peg
   crawling peg
10. Eurodollars
11. Forward exchange

Answers to True–False Questions

1. F
2. T
3. F
4. T
5. T
6. F
7. F
8. F
9. F
10. F
11. T
12. F
13. F
14. F
15. T
16. T
17. T
18. T
19. T
20. F
21. T
22. F

Answers to Multiple-Choice Questions

1. a
2. a
3. d
4. c
5. a
6. b
7. e
8. a
9. d
10. a
11. c
12. c
13. c
14. d

CHAPTER 23

The Challenge of Economic Development

CHAPTER ORIENTATION

This chapter develops and explains the following concepts:

Characteristics of less developed countries, and the meaning of economic development.

The five stages that tend to characterize the growth of nations as they progress from underdeveloped to fully developed status.

The factors requisite to economic development, such as agricultural development and reform, population control, and investment in both physical and human capital.

The advantages and disadvantages of investment in capital-intensive versus labor-intensive projects, and in large versus small projects.

The measurement of return on investment, and the difference between private and social profitability.

Private foreign investment and foreign aid, two means by which a less developed country can acquire investment from abroad.

FILL-IN QUESTIONS

Complete the following sentences. (Answers are given at the end of the chapter.)

1. Countries that tend to be characterized by poverty, high rates of population growth, low proportions of adult literacy, and a large majority of the labor force employed in agriculture are called _____

   _____ .

2. _____

   exists when employed resources are not being used in their most efficient ways.

3. _____

   refers to the process whereby a nation's real per capita output or income increases over a long period of time.

4. The economic and social overhead capital of a nation needed as a basis for modern production is called its

   _____ .

5. _____ consists of loans, grants, or assistance by one government to another for the purpose of accelerating economic development in the recipient country.

6. The agency established in 1944 to provide loans and credit for postwar reconstruction and to promote development of poorer countries is the _____

_____

_____

_____ .

SELF-TEST: TRUE–FALSE QUESTIONS

Circle T if the statement is true, F if it is false. (Answers are given at the end of the chapter.)

T F 1. Disguised unemployment may refer to the inefficient utilization of employed labor.

T F 2. LDCs tend to export a wide variety of items in order to obtain foreign exchange.

T F 3. A country whose GNP has increased by 20 percent over a decade must have been, by definition, undergoing economic development.

T F 4. Although many countries have been experiencing economic development, the gap between the richest and the poorest countries has, in fact, been increasing.

T F 5. Studies of economically advanced countries have shown that economic development can be divided into five distinct stages, and one stage does not begin until the previous one clearly has been completed.

T F 6. In the development of LDCs, growth in the industrial sector appears to be strongly influenced by technical progress in the agricultural sector.

T F 7. It has been found that land reform by itself has been overwhelmingly successful in raising farm productivity.

T F 8. Studies have indicated that it is cheaper to increase real income per capita by reducing population growth than by building new factories.

T F 9. The marginal productivity of capital is likely to be high in LDCs because they have so little capital relative to labor.

T F 10. The amount of new capital an LDC can utilize effectively is dependent on both the availability of related skilled labor and effective demand for the output of the new capital.

T F 11. Even in LDCs, the marginal productivity of certain types of labor may be quite high.

T F 12. Many LDCs would probably benefit more from an increase in middle-level skills than from an increase in high-level skills.

T F 13. Reducing mortality rates in LDCs would, in and of itself, be very helpful in raising GNP per capita.

T F 14. It is pointless for an LDC to concern itself with the labor-intensity versus capital-intensity criterion when deciding whcih types of industry it should promote.

T F 15. As a general rule in LDCs, the private rate of return on investment projects exceeds the social rate of return.

T F 16. Developed countries have all been exceedingly reluctant to loan funds to LDCs for the purpose of developing infrastructure facilities.

T F 17. The Agency for International Development administers the use of funds voted by Congress for economic, technical, and defense assistance to nations identified with the free world.

T F 18. Economists agree that aid to LDCs should normally take the form of loans rather than grants because loans are used more productively.

SELF-TEST: MULTIPLE-CHOICE QUESTIONS

Circle the letter that corresponds to the best answer. (Answers are given at the end of the chapter.)

1. Which of the following is *not* a characteristic common to most LDCs?
   (a) A high rate of population growth.
   (b) A large land area.
   (c) A low proportion of adult literacy.
   (d) Heavy reliance on one or a few items for export.
   (e) Extensive disguised unemployment.

2. According to Rostow, which of the stages of development

tends to be characterized by the adoption of modern technology and a rapidly rising state of net investment?
- (a) Stage 1: Traditional Society.
- (b) Stage 2: Preconditions for Takeoff.
- (c) Stage 3: Takeoff.
- (d) Stage 4: Drive to Maturity.
- (e) Stage 5: Maturity.

3. Which of the stages of development tends to be characterized by the economy assuming a significant role in world trade, a high rate of investment, and a rate of growth in output greater than in population?
- (a) Stage 1.
- (b) Stage 2.
- (c) Stage 3.
- (d) Stage 4.
- (e) Stage 5.

4. Studies have shown that land reform:
- (a) Cannot be achieved.
- (b) Has always been overwhelmingly successful in increasing agricultural productivity.
- (c) Is not related to agricultural productivity.
- (d) Is helpful only when land is fragmented into many small, independent units.
- (e) May reduce productivity unless accompanied by the implementation of new techniques and increased availability of credit.

5. According to studies on the effectiveness of capital in promoting economic development:
- (a) Capital and development are not related.
- (b) Capital cannot be absorbed efficiently by LDCs in unlimited amounts in any short period of time.
- (c) Capital can always be efficiently absorbed by LDCs.
- (d) Capital can be absorbed efficiently in large amounts by LDCs if the population is growing very quickly.
- (e) Infusions of foreign capital often slow down the development process.

6. When investing in human capital, LDCs should *not* attempt to
- (a) Emphasize basic technical training.
- (b) Develop primarily high-level skills.
- (c) Utilize foreign experts in domestic education and training.
- (d) Invest in public health.
- (e) Reduce population growth through the disemination of birth control information.

7. With regard to labor-intensive versus capital-intensive projects:
- (a) Labor-intensive projects are always preferable.

(b) Capital-intensive projects are always preferable.
- (c) Labor-intensive projects are preferable whenever capital is redundant.
- (d) Factor intensity if often not a useful criterion for making investment decisions within an industry.
- (e) Factor intensity is never a useful criterion when used to compare potential interindustry investments.

8. The private rate of return differs from the social rate of return in that:
- (a) The private rate of return is a net return, whereas the social rate of return is not.
- (b) The social rate of return is a net return, whereas the private rate of return is not.
- (c) The private rate of return is not necessarily calculated using market values, whereas the social rate of return is.
- (d) The private rate of return always exceeds the social rate of return in LDCs.
- (e) The social rate of return may take into account many nonmarket factors which the private rate of return does not.

9. Which of the following makes the *least* sense when attempting to attract private foreign investment into a country?
- (a) Permitting foreign corporations to invest only in projects with a high social rate of return.
- (b) Insuring foreign corporations against loss due to destruction of their property.
- (c) Providing foreign corporations with nonnationalization guarantees.
- (d) Permitting foreign corporations to transfer some profit out of LDCs.
- (e) Giving foreign corporations tax concessions.

10. Economists prefer a program approach to a project approach to aid because:
- (a) Projects often are not carefully enough defined.
- (b) Programs permit greater flexibility.
- (c) Programs do not have to be carefully administered.
- (d) Programs tend to be cheaper.
- (e) Programs tend to be more labor intensive.

11. With regard to the loans versus grants controversy, a reasonable policy guide would be:
- (a) When in doubt, make loans because they are generally more effective.
- (b) When in doubt, give grants because they are generally more effective.
- (c) Give grants to richer countries, loans to poorer ones.
- (d) Give grants to poorer countries, loans to richer ones.
- (e) Give neither if the recipient country has a balance-of-payments deficit.

At this point you should be able to do all of the following:

1. Define all of the technical terms and concepts listed at the end of the chapter in the text.

2. Describe the general position of LDCs with respect to:
   (a) Income, saving, and capital accumulation.
   (b) Population.
   (c) The degree of industrialization.
   (d) The efficiency of resource utilization.

3. Describe the five stages of economic development through which, according to W. W. Rostow, nations pass, and discuss two shortcomings of this theory.

4. Explain why growth of the industrial sector tends to be influenced by technical progress in the agricultural sector.

5. Discuss the degree to which land reform alone has been effective in promoting agricultural development, and describe other measures that ought to accompany land reform.

6. Explain how population growth affects economic development.

7. Explain why economists used to think that the answer to economic development was "more capital," and why this view has been modified in more recent years.

8. Discuss the types of investment in human capital that are needed in LDCs to promote development.

9. Define and discuss the logic behind the labor-intensity and capital-intensity criteria for investment programs, and explain the usefulness of criteria such as these.

10. Discuss the relative merits of small-scale and large-scale investment projects for LDCs.

11. Explain why the private and social rates of return on an investment project may differ, and how such rates may be useful guides to investment decisions.

12. Describe several measures that underdeveloped countries might undertake to attract private foreign investment.

13. Describe the chief functions of the International Bank for Reconstruction and Development and the Agency for International Development (AID).

14. Discuss briefly each of the following issues with regard to foreign aid:
    (a) Providing aid for specific projects rather than general programs.
    (b) The "right" amount of aid to give.
    (c) Restrictions on foreign aid.
    (d) Giving loans rather than grants.

QUESTIONS TO THINK ABOUT

1. In what ways would studying the development of now-advanced nations help in devising a program of development for LDCs? Could application of the knowledge regarding the development of advanced nations ever be harmful?

2. Do you think that there is only one path of development, or could an LDC develop in different ways?

3. Why do you think that the gap between the economically advanced nations and the LDCs tends to widen over time?

4. Why don't LDCs simply borrow technology and money from the advanced nations and develop? In other words, is there more to development than just money and knowledge?

5. Are there any economic reasons that advanced countries such as the United States should want the LDCs to develop?

6. What benefits, economic and otherwise, does the United States get from giving foreign aid? In what ways, if any, might such aid be detrimental to the United States?

7. If you were an economic adviser to an LDC and were considering the relative advantages of investing in a steel mill or in a telephone system, what factors would you consider in making the investment decision?

ANSWERS

Answers to Fill-in Questions

1. less developed countries
2. Disguised unemployment
3. Economic development
4. infrastructure
5. Foreign aid
6. International Bank for Reconstruction and Development

Answers to True–False Questions

1. T
2. F
3. F
4. T
5. F
6. T
7. F
8. T
9. T
10. T
11. T
12. T
13. F
14. F
15. F
16. F
17. T
18. F

Answers to Multiple-Choice Questions

1. b
2. c
3. d
4. e
5. b
6. b
7. d
8. e
9. a
10. b
11. d

CHAPTER 24

Economic Planning:
The Visible Hand in Mixed
and in Command Economies

CHAPTER ORIENTATION

This chapter develops and explains the following concepts:

Economic planning, its goals, and two analytical tools of planning: econometric models and input–output analysis.

The nature of Soviet economic institutions and planning.

Some reforms which the U.S.S.R. has introduced to encourage greater efficiency, and the accomplishments and failures of Soviet planning.

The evolution of new social and economic systems in China, and the objectives of these systems.

Planning in China, and some of its accomplishments.

The convergence hypothesis, which proposes the eventual merging of capitalistic and communistic systems.

FILL-IN QUESTIONS

Complete the following sentences. (Answers are given at the end of the chapter.)

1. A(n) _____ is a detailed scheme, formulated beforehand, for achieving specific objectives by governing the activities and inter-relationships of those economic organisms that have an influence on the desired outcome.

2. An economic system in which the government directs resources for the purpose of deciding what, how, and possibly for whom to produce is called a(n) _____ _____ .

3. _____ expresses economic relationships in the form of mathematical equations and verifies resulting models by statistical methods.

4. In the U.S.S.R., _____ are agricultural lands owned and operated as state enterprises under government-appointed managing directors, whereas _____ are communities of farmers who pool their resources, lease land from the government, and divide the profits among their members.

5. _____

_____

is a technical term used in the Soviet Union to mean the

expected percent rate of return on a capital investment.

6. When employed resources are not being used in their most

efficient ways, _____

is said to exist.

7. The theory which proposes that capitalism and communism

will eventually merge to form a new kind of society, in

which the personal freedoms and profit motive of Western

capitalistic democracies blend with the government controls

that exist in communistic economies, is called _____

_____

_____.

SELF-TEST: TRUE–FALSE QUESTIONS

*Circle T if the statement is true, F if it is false. (Answers
are given at the end of the chapter.)*

T F 1. Economic plans are necessary and useful only
in command economies.

T F 2. Technical efficiency is a primary goal of
planned economies, but economic efficiency
need not be.

T F 3. Econometric models, although developed, have
not yet been used for planning by any country.

T F 4. Econometric models may be used to ascertain
the likely results of different policy actions.

T F 5. One problem with input–output analysis is that
the tables used for prediction are derived from
past rather than current or expected future
relationships in the economy.

T F 6. The U.S.S.R. today defines its economic system
as communistic.

T F 7. Collective farming is the dominant form of
agriculture in the U.S.S.R.

T F 8. Collective farms sell the bulk of their output on
the private market and turn the proceeds over
to the state.

T F 9. In the U.S.S.R., every worker is paid the same
wage.

T F 10. In the U.S.S.R., people have much the same
freedoms of consumer and occupational choice
as do people in the United States.

T F 11. In the U.S.S.R. the main source of revenue to
the state is the income tax.

T F 12. The greatest successes that the U.S.S.R. has had
are in the area of agriculture.

T F 13. The CRE is a measure conceptually related to the
market rate of interest (MRI).

T F 14. A plan in the U.S.S.R. tends, because of
bureaucratic problems, to be a rigid once-and-for-
all arrangement.

T F 15. A major problem of planning in the U.S.S.R.
is to achieve balance in the sense that enough
of each required input is produced in order to
produce targeted amounts of different outputs.

T F 16. The Soviet economy has had a better record
of maintaining high employment than has the
United States, but its problem with inflation
has been more serious.

T F 17. The U.S.S.R. has achieved a remarkable degree
of efficiency in the allocation of its resources.

T F 18. China's ideology is a blend of Marxism and
Maoism.

T F 19. The primary goal of China's leadership is rapid
economic development.

T F 20. Although the Chinese economy is economically
inefficient, it is technically efficient.

T F 21. In the early 1970s China finally achieved a perfectly equal distribution of income.

T F 22. With the growth experienced by both the
United States and the U.S.S.R. over the last
several decades, it is increasingly clear that the
convergence hypothesis is correct.

SELF-TEST: MULTIPLE-CHOICE QUESTIONS

*Circle the letter that corresponds to the best answer.
(Answers are given at the end of the chapter.)*

1. Input–output analysis can predict:
(a) What will happen to demand for specified products in
the future.

(b) What will happen to the unemployment rate several years in the future.
(c) What will happen to prices of specified commodities if the demand for them changes.
(d) What will happen to the demand for the output of all industries when the demand for the output of a specific industry changes.
(e) What will happen to the supplies of various resources when their prices change.

2. Which of the following is a main reason that scientific planning techniques have come to be used increasingly over the years?
(a) The realization that without planning economies cannot function well.
(b) The discovery that only planned economies tend to operate with both technical and economic efficiency.
(c) The rapid advance of computer science, facilitating the processing of large quantities of data.
(d) The increased availability of information about economic interrelationships that will exist in the future.
(e) The realization that growth and stability are achievable only if controls are placed on economic systems.

3. In the U.S.S.R. today:
(a) All people must work for the state.
(b) People can work for themselves but, with few exceptions, cannot hire labor.
(c) All goods are publicly owned.
(d) Consumer goods but not consumer durables such as automobiles and houses are privately owned.
(e) All savings are appropriated by the state.

4. One difference between state farms and collective farms is that:
(a) The former are owned by individual farmers, whereas the latter are collectively owned.
(b) The former operate on land leased from the state, whereas the latter operate on collevtively owned land.
(c) The former are managed by the farmers themselves, whereas the latter are managed by professionals.
(d) The former pay set wages to labor, whereas the latter divide whatever profits are made among members.
(e) The former are the dominant type of agricultural organization, whereas the latter are becoming less important over time.

5. Which of the following is true of the U.S.S.R.?
(a) There is freedom of consumer choice but there is not consumer sovereignty.
(b) There is consumer sovereignty but there is no freedom of consumer choice.

(c) There is neither consumer sovereignty nor freedom of consumer choice.
(d) There is both consumer sovereignty and freedom of consumer choice.
(e) There is consumer sovereignty and freedom of consumer choice with regard to consumer goods but not with regard to capital goods.

6. Taxes in the U.S.S.R.:
(a) Do not exist.
(b) Exist but are very low.
(c) Are set at moderate levels in order to provide revenue for the state.
(d) Are considerably higher than they are in the United States as a percent of GNP.
(e) Are based almost entirely on personal income.

7. Which of the following has *not* been an objective of Soviet planning?
(a) To make a large number of LDCs economically dependent on U.S.S.R. exports.
(b) To attain the highest per capita output in the world.
(c) To build a major military complex.
(d) To provide health and educational facilities to all.
(e) To achieve economic self-sufficiency with respect to the outside world.

8. In the preparation of an output plan in the U.S.S.R.:
(a) The government is not concerned with consumer preferences.
(b) The government attempts to measure the real cost of all labor and nonlabor costs of production.
(c) The government does not attempt to include in its cost calculations all costs associated with production and distribution.
(d) The government does not worry about labor costs, since labor can be obtained by decree.
(e) The government does not worry about costs since it can guide the economy in any desired direction.

9. With regard to growth in the U.S.S.R. relative to growth in the United States:
(a) Real GNP has grown faster in the United States since the 1960s.
(b) Real GNP grew faster in the United States in the 1950s but slower in the 1960s.
(c) Although real GNP has grown faster in the U.S.S.R. since the 1950s, its relative rate of increase has declined.
(d) Although real GNP has grown faster in the United States, its relative rate of increase has accelerated.
(e) There is no way of comparing growth in the two countries because GNP in each is defined differently.

10. Which of the following statements about income distribution in the U.S.S.R. is correct?
    (a) Income is equally distributed.
    (b) Income is equitably distributed according to the needs standard.
    (c) Income is *not* distributed in accordance with the contributive standard.
    (d) Income is more equally distributed in the U.S.S.R. than it is in mixed economies.
    (e) Income is not distributed; goods and services are.

11. Which of the following has *not*, at one time or another, been a Soviet reform aimed at increasing overall efficiency?
    (a) Increased use of advertising.
    (b) Extensive use of the free market to allocate capital between the consumer and government sectors of the economy.
    (c) The use of bonuses for workers as an incentive for greater efficiency.
    (d) Increased decentralization of decision making.
    (e) The use of price reductions in marketing programs to increase sales of certain products.

12. Which of the following concerning the goals of modern China is *not* true?
    (a) A classless society.
    (b) Minimal individualistic orientation.
    (c) Public ownership of all resources.
    (d) An altruistic society.
    (e) Distribution in accordance with the contributive standard.

13. China's economy is organized in such a way as to facilitate:
    (a) Centralized economic planning.
    (b) Distribution according to the contribution of each worker to production.
    (c) The operation of supply and demand so as to encourage efficient allocation of resources.
    (d) The development of small private enterprises.
    (e) Efficiency in the use of all resources.

14. The only significant type of income payment in China is:
    (a) Wages.
    (b) Rent.
    (c) Interest.
    (d) Profit.
    (e) Transfer payments.

15. Which of the following has China *not* commonly used to achieve economic stability and growth?
    (a) Economic incentives such as bonuses and gifts to encourage worker productivity.
    (b) Worker participation in decision making.
    (c) Use of increased profits for capital investment.

    (d) Monetary and fiscal policies geared toward maintaining price stability.
    (e) A low-wage, high-profit, heavy-investment orientation.

CHECKPOINT: LEARNING OBJECTIVES

At this point, you should be able to do all of the following:

1. Define all of the technical terms and concepts listed at the end of the chapter in the text.

2. Explain what is meant by each of the following goals of planning:
   (a) Efficiency.
   (b) Equity.
   (c) Stability and growth.

3. Describe what an econometric model is, and explain how both forecasting and simulating with a model are useful for planning.

4. Explain what input–output analysis is and how an input–output table is useful in forecasting and planning.

5. Describe some shortcomings of input–output analysis.

6. State the degree to which private ownership exists today in the U.S.S.R. and the degree to which industry and trade are under state control.

7. Describe the difference between state and collective farms.

8. Describe the two main types of economic incentives used in the U.S.S.R. to encourage high productivity and an acceptable distribution of labor among different types of jobs.

9. Explain the difference between consumer sovereignty and consumer choice, and state which exists in the U.S.S.R.

10. Describe the types of money and the main sources of tax revenue in the U.S.S.R.

11. Explain the problems of "balance" and "flexibility" in economic planning.

12. Describe the major objectives of the Soviet five-year plans.

13. Explain why, in establishing output plans, government leaders must be concerned with consumer preferences and relative production costs, and describe how the leaders appear to measure these costs.

14. Explain how planners determine which potential investment projects to undertake.

15. Describe some reorganizations and changes which the Soviet Union has introduced in order to encourage greater

efficiency, and state why these reforms have met with only limited success.

16. Describe the major accomplishments and failures of Soviet economic planning with regard to growth, stability, equity, and efficiency.

17. Describe the ideological goals of China's leaders.

18. Describe the organization of China's industrial and agricultural sectors, and explain how this structure facilitates centralized economic planning.

19. Discuss two ways in which the Chinese economy is not efficient.

20. Discuss how income is distributed in China, and describe the degree to which equality has been achieved.

21. Describe how China uses each of the following in an attempt to achieve economic stability:
    (a) Incentives.
    (b) A wage-price policy.
    (c) Fiscal-monetary controls.

22. State two reasons why China's low-wage policy encourages economic growth.

23. Describe the convergence hypothesis, state the basic assumptions on which it rests, and explain whether or not convergence is likely to become a reality.

QUESTIONS TO THINK ABOUT

1. Assume that you are a planner in the U.S.S.R. and are asked how many laborers should be sent to mine coal next year. How would you go about making this calculation? What types of factors would you consider? Would an econometric model be useful to you? An input–output table?

2. Why do you suppose that soviet economic growth has been faster than U.S. economic growth?

3. In what ways would the development of computer technology help economic planning?

4. Democracy and planning can be consistent. Explain how you would go about devising a "Democratic Five-Year Plan."

5. Can planning do anything for an economy that the market mechanism cannot do? Can the market mechanism do anything for an economy that planning cannot do?

6. "Since the U.S.S.R. has been placing more reliance on economic indicators and incentives, and the United States has been placing greater importance on the role of the government in the economy, convergence is inevitable." Do you agree?

ANSWERS

Answers to Fill-in Questions

1. economic plan
2. planned economy
3. econometrics
4. state farms
   collective farms
5. Coefficient of relative effectiveness
6. underemployment
7. the convergence hypothesis

Answers to True–False Questions

1. F
2. T
3. F
4. T
5. T
6. F
7. T
8. F
9. F
10. T
11. F
12. F
13. F
14. F
15. T
16. F
17. F
18. T
19. F
20. F
21. F
22. F

Answers to Multiple-Choice Questions

1. d
2. c
3. b
4. d
5. a
6. d
7. a
8. c
9. c
10. d
11. b
12. e
13. a
14. a
15. a